It should be no secret that deep friendships are one of the great mysteries and missing pieces in the lives of most pastors. Although many desire close relationships, ministry provides unique challenges that can make the pursuit of them risky and painful. Haykin, Croft, and Carroll offer gospel-grounded help for pastors who desperately need friends, and the good fruit that God provides through them.

**Ronnie Martin**
Lead Pastor of Substance Church, Ashland, Ohio
Author of *The God Who Is With Us*

Friendship is something often discussed but rarely understood. This is especially true for *pastors*. As shepherds to God's sheep and heralds of God's Word, they are often those who feel like they cannot make friends or have deep, lasting friendships. Brian, Michael, and James bring a balm of good news to those fears. Let these men—themselves exemplars of godly, kind, and persistent friends—remind you why it is both important for your ministry but also for your own soul. You *need* friends. You are your best self, and so you are the best shepherd to God's people, when deep abiding friendships mark your life. If that is not you, let these men take a gentle hand to your shoulder and say to you, 'Come alongside, friend, and let us help you see.' This book is a treasure for a pastor and for those that love them, especially as their friends.

**Bryan Baise**
Associate Professor of Philosophy and Apologetics,
Boyce College, Louisville, Kentucky
Professor,

T0016968

We live in a time of rich access to great theological writings, but in one way that I fear our generation of Christians, including and perhaps especially the pastors, is quite impoverished. That is in the area of friendship. We have too readily absorbed the radical individualism of our culture, and then wonder why we are lonely and overburdened. This book is a biblical, historical, and practical study of friendship for Christian leaders that I hope will be widely read and deeply.

**Joel R. Beeke**
President, Puritan Reformed Theological Seminary,
Grand Rapids, Illinois

This is a stirring and much-needed reminder that to survive the struggles of ministry—especially the draining duties of countering false teaching in the church—pastors need the blessings that can only flow through godly spiritual friendships. This book convincingly demonstrates from scripture and from history how loyal, supportive companionship (not just 'excessive acquaintanceship') can build resilience through the rigors of battle, and perseverance amidst the storms and isolating pressures of ministry. Get the book, and cherish your friends.

**Lee Gatiss**
Director of Church Society and author of
*Light After Darkness: How the Reformers Regained, Retold, and Relied on the Gospel of Grace*

Every so often a book comes across my desk which makes me sit up and take notice. This book, dealing with a much-neglected aspect of pastoral life and ministry, is one of those.

Haykin, Croft and Carroll examine and commend the virtue and blessing of friendship. Drawing upon familiar scriptural and less well-known historical examples and employing theological categories, the subject is explored with clarity, warmth and practical appeal. Nuggets of wisdom appear everywhere in these pages, for example: 'In contrast to the comparative uselessness of acquaintances, the true friend mirrors a brother in terms of commitment during difficulty' (p. 103). The authors recognise the challenges in cultivating such friendship but, at the same time, convincingly promote its blessings as reflecting what it means to be truly human and authentically Christian.

This is a book I recommend to all Christian leaders no matter their vintage, but especially to young pastors and those in training for the pastoral office.

**Edwin Ewart**
Principal, Irish Baptist College, Moira, Northern Ireland

Because friendship is a neglected subject in pastoral leadership development, it comes as no surprise that too many pastors are isolated in ministry, lacking deep, meaningful friendships. This book should be mandatory reading for leadership classes in our seminaries. Dear pastors, for the good of your soul, do not merely take up and read this excellent work; develop intimate friendships as a result!

**Ryan Rippee**
President, The Cornerstone Bible College and Seminary,
Vallejo, California
Pastor, Trinity Church of Benicia, Benicia, California

# PASTORAL FRIENDSHIP

## THE FORGOTTEN PIECE TO A PERSEVERING MINISTRY

MICHAEL A. G. HAYKIN, BRIAN CROFT & JAMES B. CARROLL

CHRISTIAN
FOCUS

Copyright © Michael A.G. Haykin, Brian Croft
and James B. Carroll 2022

paperback ISBN 978-1-5271-0916-2
ebook ISBN 978-1-5271-0955-1

First published in 2022
by
Christian Focus Publications Ltd, Geanies House,
Fearn, Ross-shire, IV20 1TW, Scotland
www.christianfocus.com
with
Practical Shepherding, Inc, P.O. Box 21806, Louisville, Kentucky 40221, USA
www.practicalshepherding.com

A CIP catalogue record for this book is available from the
British Library.

Cover design by James Amour

Printed and bound by Bell & Bain, Glasgow.

# Contents

To the men who have helped us persevere by befriending us. Thank you.

# FOREWORD

It is an honor and a privilege to be invited to write the foreword to this book. Two of its authors I count as valued friends. Over the years, I have discovered that there are those who want to be friendly, but comparatively few who want to be open and transparent, sharing in the deepest interests of others. Then sadly, there are those who begin as friends but inflict disappointment and pain by proving to be unfaithful friends.

Some years ago I was attending a pastors' fraternal. In the discussion that followed the preaching, the subject of friendships became a focal point. I cannot recall all the details now, but I recall my stressing the vital importance of pastors having real friends in order to preserve both our sanity and usefulness. Over the years I have met some pastors who seemed aloof, were prickly and difficult to engage in conversation, or who seemed eccentric and at various points unbalanced in some of their opinions. They did not always display clear thinking or act wisely. I found out later that in many cases they had few, if any, real friends.

It has been said, 'Tell me about your friends and I will tell you who you are.' Prior to that fraternal I had read *Friends of Calvin* by Machiel A. van den Berg and was impressed by the number and variety of friends whose company Calvin enjoyed and on whom he could rely. Calvin would never have been the kind of person he was in Geneva without the friendships of men like William Farel, Martin Bucer, Heinrich Bullinger, Phillip Melanchthon, Theodore Beza, and Pierre Viret among others. One of his very best friends was Pierre Viret from Lausanne. A special bond existed between them, evident in their correspondence. Reading that book drove home to me the absolute necessity and value of loyal and trusted friends in the ministry.

Isolation is a very real temptation and a great danger to any pastor. Some might say 'it goes with the job' and resign themselves to a life of loneliness. David was familiar with loneliness. At times he felt himself to be 'a stranger in the earth' (Ps. 119:19 NKJV). Yet he knew where to find real friends, 'I am a companion of all who fear You' (Ps. 119:63 NKJV). God, in His wisdom and goodness, provides such companions for His servants. One of Satan's ploys is to isolate the man of God and if possible to drive him to despair and reduce his effectiveness as a pastor. Sadly, it is even possible to become isolated from your closest companion, your own wife, let alone men who might be a particular help and encouragement to you.

*Pastoral Friendship* is an invaluable book and different from other books I have read on friendships. Drawing on what to me were unknown friendships (apart from Charles Spurgeon and Archibald Brown), and then unfolding the basis, the blessings, and challenges to friendship, the authors provide a firm, incisive, and compelling biblical and practical rationale for cultivating true friendships. They conclude with ten penetrating exhortations to their readers.

Having served as a pastor in Sussex, England for over four decades I look back with gratitude to God for those who bore with my quirks and foibles and yet became long-standing loyal friends. Some of them were my peers, others were older than me, some younger. A few were not pastors but wise men. Some of my pastoral friends were in the UK and others in the USA. Now I have retired I still maintain these friendships and have added a few more. These men were the ones I turned to when faced with crises in the church. Others I might simply ask about how to interpret a difficult passage of Scripture, or to work through a particular issue. Often it would be to pray together or simply to share some of the everyday things of life, enjoying a coffee and a chat or enjoying a meal together. With options like Facetime and other social media now readily available it is not always necessary to actually meet at the same location.

Those friends have, by their counsel, kept me sane, have comforted and provoked me, challenged and rebuked me when necessary. They have helped me to think more clearly and act more wisely. I hope I have been a good friend to others. True friendships are of mutual benefit – being a good listener as well as a good counsellor.

I am pleased to see the too-often neglected subject of pastoral friendships addressed in what follows. No one ever told me about their necessity at seminary over fifty years ago. My prayer is that this book will become a source of instruction and encouragement to all God's servants but especially those who are setting out to be faithful preachers of God's Word and pastors of God's flock. *Tolle lege.*

Austin Walker[1]

Former Pastor (Retired), Maidenbower Baptist Church,
Crawley, England

Author, *The Excellent Benjamin Keach* and
*God's Care for the Widow*

---

1. Austin is now 'retired' after over forty years of pastoral ministry and living in the East Midlands with his wife Mai. He is the author of several books, occasional preacher, and one who relishes friendships with loyal and trusted friends. He also co-wrote a Practical Shepherding book with Brian Croft entitled, *Caring for Widows* (Crossway 2015).

# INTRODUCTION

## SPURGEON AND BROWN

Charles Spurgeon (1834–1892) is one of our heroes. We love so many of the same things about Spurgeon that others commonly love about him: his Christ-centered preaching, wit, humor, courage, authenticity, boldness, brilliance, and ministry faithfulness, to name a few. However, the more we learn about this prince of preachers, the more we feel drawn to some of the lesser-known qualities of this larger-than-life figure. As a very young pastor, he was one of the few pastors willing to go into the homes of those infected by the plague in London and care for the sick and dying. He was uniquely transparent about his struggles with depression. And another lesser-known mark of Spurgeon we have come to admire was his close, intimate friendships with other men—particularly pastors.

Iain Murray wrote a biography on Spurgeon's eventual successor, Archibald Brown (1844–1922). Brown pastored another large congregation on the other side of London from Spurgeon. There are a few moments in the book where Murray beautifully captures the sweet friendship that existed between Brown and Spurgeon. One aspect of Brown's suffering was the loss of two different wives within a few years of each other. Upon the despair and grief Brown experienced just days after the death of his second wife, Brown later wrote about Spurgeon's care of him:

> Broken with sore grief, I went over to the Metropolitan Tabernacle. I could not preach but I thought I could worship, and how amazed I was to find that he had prepared a sermon on purpose for me ... As I turned round to come out at the close of the service, there was just one grip of his hand as he said, 'I have done all I can for you, my poor fellow.' I felt he had. I rode home with him that day, and had his loving fellowship as he sat with me during the afternoon.[1]

Years later when Spurgeon was just a few weeks from his own death, he penned this final letter to Brown:

> Beloved Brother, receive the assurance of my heart-love, although you need no such assurance from me. You have long been most dear to me; but in your standing shoulder to shoulder with me in protest against deadly error we have become more than ever one. The Lord sustain, comfort, perfect you! Debtors to free and sovereign grace, we will together sing to our redeeming Lord, world without end.[2]

---

1. Iain H. Murray, *Archibald G. Brown: Spurgeon's Successor* (Edinburgh: Banner of Truth, 2011), p. 98.

2. Murray, *Archibald G. Brown*, p.144.

News of Spurgeon's death reached Brown in London one day after his death. In Brown's sermon that next Sunday at his church, he emotionally spoke about his dear friend who recently went to glory:

> He has been to me a very Elijah, and I have loved in any way possible to minister to him. Our roots have been intertwined for well nigh thirty years. Is it any wonder that I feel almost powerless this morning to think of him as a preacher, as an orator, as an organizer, or as anything except the dearest friend I have ever known.[3]

Spurgeon and Brown were spiritual giants of their day, pastoring two of the largest churches in all of England. And yet, they both knew there was something they needed to survive the rigors of ministry and the personal suffering of their life—friendship. Not just any friendship, but a close, personal, intimate, and sacrificial pastor-to-pastor friendship that regularly turned each other's gaze to Jesus.[4]

This book seeks to persuade every modern pastor of the essential need of this kind of friendship. It is a need that touches the deepest parts of the human soul, including pastors. And it is a need that is not simply rooted in enjoyment and companionship, but in the necessity to care well for one's soul and survive a long-term ministry. Pastoral friendship is the forgotten piece to a persevering ministry.

---

3. Murray, *Archibald G. Brown*, p. 145.

4. Part of this introduction was first published in *The Pastor's Soul* (Evangelical Press).

## What is Friendship?

Let us start with a basic definition of friendship. In the midst of many long, thoughtful, word-smithed definitions of friendship throughout history, here is our short, succinct description:

> Friendship is an intimate relationship of love, trust, and loyalty.

Here are a couple of presumed necessary observations as you initially process this definition. First, we recognize a relationship between two Christians will have layers of meaning and benefits that do not exist in the closest of friendships not rooted in Christ. Meaningful friendship can and does exist with unbelievers, but most would acknowledge the natural limitations of closeness in those relationships. This definition assumes the deepest experience of friendship happens between those who know and follow Jesus. This assumption will be nuanced more throughout the book.

Second, you may have caught a certain word choice that makes some men uncomfortable. The phrase, 'intimate relationship' was a carefully chosen word to round out this definition. Many, in both our secular and Christian cultural movements, have wrongfully positioned the word 'intimate' to exclusively imply sexual connection. That can be an aspect of intimacy, but if we dig into the basic definition of 'intimate' it speaks of being 'familiar and close' with another human being. With this intentional definition, we seek to recover a proper meaning and usefulness of what it means to be truly 'familiar, close, and known' by someone else in the context of friendship. We trust it will be particularly helpful once we draw the connection to the blessings and benefit of friendship among pastors.

It will be this simple, yet compact definition of friendship that will nuance the argument we seek to make with this book. That is:

> Spirit-empowered friendship enables pastors and those under their care to flourish.

Every modern pastor needs the presence and friendship of other pastors to thrive and persevere throughout the unique challenges of pastoral ministry. We seek to convince pastors of this through two key parts. First, we want to begin with Scripture and church history. Chapter one will focus on some of the key friendships we find in both the Old and New Testaments. We will seek to do this while specifically highlighting how the wisdom and insight of the book of Proverbs create a framework to understand biblical friendship.

We then trust that God's design for pastoral friendship will come to life through examining history. By examining meaningful friendships between pastors from the past in chapters two and three, we are confident they will be an inspiration and guide to teach us how modern pastors can pursue the same thing—experiencing many of the same benefits. This also allows an opportunity to peek behind the curtain of the lives of some of our lesser-known pastoral heroes to learn from their example.

Second, we want to apply God's truth and design for friendship to the modern pastor. Chapters four through seven will take these insights from Scripture and the patterns of our pastoral heroes from the past and press us forward to consider the obstacles and challenges, as well as the benefits of friendship among pastors. Much of this, particularly the final chapter, will be rooted in our own experiences as well as the blessings we each have received through our own friendship with other pastors—as well as each other.

## A Final Caveat

One last word before you begin. The importance of this book is merely a piece into a broader theme in the life of a pastor—the care for his own soul. There is an incredible irony with pastors. Pastors dedicate their whole life and ministry to the serving and pouring out for the good of the souls of others, at the detriment of their own soul. And in many cases, pastors assume the neglect of their own souls is simply part of the call of God on their life. Inevitably, this explains why 50 per cent of pastors will leave the ministry in five years and a staggering 80 per cent will leave in ten years.

Therefore, this book is important not simply so pastors can have meaningful fellowship and 'intimate' masculine companionship throughout the challenges of ministry. But this book highlights one of several means of grace God has provided for pastors to care for their own soul, as they care for the souls of others (Heb. 13:17). And ultimately, it is the pastors' priority to care for their own souls that will keep them in the ministry for the long haul. Or, as the Apostle Peter said to the pastors in his day, 'Shepherd the flock that is among you ... press on in it in this way ... on behalf of the Chief Shepherd until he returns for us all' (1 Peter 5:2-4 our paraphrase).

Longevity. Faithfulness. Fruitfulness. Joy in the pastor's soul as he does this work and fulfills his ministry (2 Tim. 4:5). That is our aim with this book. We pray it will work to that end.

# PART 1

# LOOKING BACK

# 1

# PORTRAITS OF FRIENDSHIPS IN SCRIPTURE

The Bible clearly teaches by direct command. We thank God for the hundreds of exhortations that most obviously direct our beliefs, thoughts, and behavior. But overt commands are not the exclusive method for instruction in Scripture. In many other places, God steers us by expounding upon, illustrating, exemplifying, and applying these commands through the positive and negative examples of real people. Take idolatry, for example. Could God be clearer than He was in Exodus 20:3-4 in the first and second commandments? Or could He make it plainer than in Paul's straightforward words to the Corinthians 'do not be idolators' and to 'flee from idolatry'?[1] And yet, God preserved the record of the history of Israel and their persistent struggle with this sin. In fact, Paul is using that narrative as the backdrop for these commands to give further nuance and clarity.

---

1. 1 Corinthians 10:7 and 10:14.

In other places, biblical narrative gathers up a number of commands by giving real-world pictures for how God's people are meant to live in His world. One such example is friendship. It would be most accurate to say that friendship is assumed in the Scriptures more than it's commanded. It's a particular manifestation of human relationship that develops for almost every person in every culture throughout history. Nearly all people have at least one friend. Of course, not all 'friendship' is the same and God designed us to enjoy His version of it. So while people will define and describe it in near-countless ways, the Bible provides a vision for true, God-honoring friendship. That's what we are commending to you in this book. To see it, however, we will look at human relationships through the prism of biblical descriptions, historical examples, and biblical commands allowing the refraction to reveal God's design. We begin with examples of friendship in the Scriptures.

## Adam and Eve

Starting at the beginning seems best, especially when searching for God's design for any aspect of His creation. While the echoes and whispers of the ideal for human relationships continue to ripple through the Scriptures, going back to Eden establishes the foundation for our understanding of friendship.

'In the beginning, God created the heavens and the earth.' As Moses recounts the creating work of God to form and fill His creation, he interjects God's approval along the way. He repeatedly assessed His handiwork as 'good.' In fact, this expression appears seven times in Genesis 1 and to the last one he adds an adverb of force or abundance, which yields the translation, 'very good.' Suffice to say, God was pleased with His creation.

Beginning in Genesis 2:4, the reader is brought back into Day 6 to learn more details related to God's creation of the first two humans. The first telling leaves the impression that God made them simultaneously or at least one right after the other. But the more detailed account clarifies. He formed Adam, placed him in the garden of Eden, gave him the boundary regarding food, and then makes the first negative assessment of His creation. Of course, the creation was 'good' so far as it was, but it was 'not good' because it was incomplete. The deficiency in man's aloneness is no sign of failure in the Creator's design; rather, it highlights that relational capacity is rooted in human nature. Thus, God satisfies this need by making for him a helper or companion. Dare we say, friend.

Genesis 2:18, then, is not an assessment of the quality of God's creation along the lines of the 'good' statements in chapter one. Instead, it offers insight into God's mind during creation that provides commentary explaining why it began with two humans and not one. While procreation results from their union, the propagation of the human race doesn't appear as the first reason for making woman. Rather, God's motivation in creating the second human is to meet the first human's 'ache' for companionship.[2]

---

2. Drew Hunter labels it the 'Edenic Ache' in *Made for Friendship* (Wheaton, IL: Crossway, 2018), p. 39.

As many have noted in studying this passage, man's relational capacity mirrors God's. Different than every other creature, mankind was given personhood.[3] While not explained or described in the creation passages, this distinction is obvious from the biblical record and our experience. Mankind is unique in that we are fundamentally dissimilar from all other animate objects in the world. Moving beyond Genesis 1–2, we can see five aspects of personhood that distinguish humans from animals: moral, mental, physical, relational, and spiritual.[4]

Morally, our conscience allows us to discern right from wrong. Dogs, for example, don't have a conscience. Mentally, we think in a more sophisticated and superior way. Birds build remarkable nests with sticks and grass, but they aren't drawing blueprints for them. Physically, our bodies are superior in form and function. Horses can outrun us, but they can't swing a hammer or build themselves a stable. Relationally, we operate differently toward one another. Bees may communicate in some ways, but they don't get married or enter into contracts. Spiritually, we relate to God in a unique way. Every aspect of creation is vitally connected to the Creator, but cats aren't praying or meeting for corporate worship.

While humans are different from the rest of creation in a number of ways, the primary focus in this book

---

3. We distinguish between personhood and 'image of God' for reasons related to the interpretation of Genesis 1–3, but this discussion seems more complex than would be helpful in this volume. Our point here stands regardless of one's understanding of these terms. For more study, see Peter J. Gentry and Stephen J. Wellum, *Kingdom through Covenants* (Wheaton, IL: Crossway, 2012), pp. 184-217.

4. These categories are drawn from an explanation of 'likeness' in Wayne Grudem, *Systematic Theology* (Grand Rapids, MI: Zondervan, 1994), pp. 445-9.

stems from our relational superiority. God places two humans in the garden not primarily for procreation, but for companionship. As we read on in Genesis 2, we're introduced to the concept of covenant marriage and realize that God gave them the gift of spiritual, relational, and sexual intimacy. Surely their marriage—as it is with all marriages—was much more than friendship, but it was never meant to be less than friendship. We know this fact because she was made to meet his need for companionship, and not strictly or primarily procreation. If friendship is an intimate relationship of love, trust, and loyalty, then it's right to use that term for their relationship. To this end, shouldn't friendship be one aspect of every marriage relationship? Even though we could say much more about the way the first two humans related to one another as husband and wife, we acknowledge the complexity of their relationship while constricting our focus to their basic companionship. Adam and Eve were friends.

Through the ups and downs of the story from Genesis 2–4, they enjoyed a relationship of love, trust, and loyalty. Just think about the fodder for their reminiscence as they neared death. They could relive the joy of God walking with them in the cool of the day and the peaceful days in Eden. They could remember with regret the episode with the serpent and lament all they forfeited. I imagine the pain of losing two sons—one to death and the other to banishment— never went away. They could recall the fresh hope of a new beginning with another son, Seth. Surely James is right that life is but a vapor, but some of those 900+ years must've dragged by. While we don't know how long Eve lived from the biblical record, she was Adam's first and surely a near-constant companion, or friend.

Among the many takeaways from the first chapters of Genesis, a few related to friendship stand out. First, our need for intimate relationships is a pre-Fall characteristic of our humanity. We need other people, and this is not a product of our fallenness. Second, human relationships were adversely affected by the Fall. The curse of conflict that descends on Adam and Eve is not restricted to them nor is it limited to marriages. Because of sin, we struggle to maintain healthy relationships. Third, close relationships continue, even under the curse of sin, to be a means of grace for God's people. They leave the garden, and based on the limited record, remain together. While it might seem odd to begin our biblical survey with Adam and Eve, they introduce us to the essential nature of our need for human relationship and thus point us toward God's design for friendship marked by intimacy, love, trust, and loyalty.

## Moses and Aaron

From spouses to siblings, we see the value and difficulty of these relationships of love, trust, and loyalty in the dominant narrative recorded in the books of Exodus and Numbers. Moses may not be on the list of the most popular baby names, but it remains a household name in popular culture in part due to the movie industry. Many older Americans associate the name with Charlton Heston while younger people think of Moses as the 'Prince of Egypt' as brought to life by Dreamworks animation. Regardless of a person's religious background, many people know the name and some pieces of his story without appreciating the full narrative or the true significance of it.

The story doesn't focus on Moses per se, but he's at the center of the story as the human leader God appointed through whom He works deliverance for His people. Leaving the more important theme of redemption aside, it's obvious that his relationships play a critical role for this strong yet frail human leader. In reading the stories involving him in the Bible, even the casual student will realize he was no lone ranger. Chief among his earthly relationships was the one between him and his older brother, Aaron.

We remember Moses' story. We meet him in Exodus 2 under the threat from Pharoah's genocidal command aimed at continuing the oppression of the Hebrews. We're told of his birth, his first three months of living in hiding, his river ride in a basket of bulrushes and bitumen, and his adoption into Egyptian royalty after being discovered by Pharoah's daughter. Fast forward forty years and Moses leaves Egypt under a cloud of suspicion after he murders an Egyptian in response to the mistreatment of a Hebrew slave. On to Midian where Moses settles into a new life, complete with a steady job and a family. After forty years on the back side of the desert, God directs him back to Egypt by speaking to him from the burning bush.

During that memorable conversation, he protests on the grounds of speaking inability. He argues that speech problems will prevent him from carrying out this divinely ordained task. God responds, 'Do you know who you're talking to? I made your mouth.'[5] Moses persists in his objection and despite His anger at Moses, God concedes, allowing him to enlist his brother, Aaron. This statement provides our introduction to Aaron, who we're told is a Levite.

Aaron is no second-rate citizen himself. He is obviously well-spoken, apparently the ranking member of the tribe of Levi,[6] a capable leader in his own right, and Moses' senior by three years. Following the exodus from Egypt, he becomes the key leader in Israel's worship as the first High Priest. Add to these descriptions, God speaks directly to Aaron in Exodus 4:27 to give him instructions even before Moses is back in town. From this reunion until their deaths forty years later, they form one legendary leadership duo. The phrase 'Moses and Aaron' appears more than sixty times in the biblical record, which only demonstrates the closeness of their ministry partnership. Moses was the front man, but Aaron is prominent in the story in both hearing from God along with Moses[7] and in doing divinely-empowered wonders before Pharoah.[8]

Think of the stories they could relive in those final days walking from Kadesh to Mount Hor. They participated in the confrontation scenes with Pharoah, the manifestations of God's power in the plagues, and the excitement of

---

5. Paraphrase of Exodus 4:11.

6. This assertion is based on the genealogy in Exodus 6:19ff.

7. Exodus 6:13; 7:6, 8; 9:8; 12:1, 43.

8. Exodus 11:10.

plundering the Egyptians on the way out. They watched God's deliverance at the Red Sea. They endured the grumbling people because of hunger and thirst. They experienced God's military deliverance from Amalek. This final episode provides one of the most vivid and lasting pictures of their co-laboring as Aaron (along with Hur) holds up Moses' arms. They ascended Mt. Sinai together. They weathered the golden calf storm, despite Aaron's role in it. They received at least portions of the Law together.[9] They led the people together for forty years in the wilderness. We have a handful of stories that confirm the ups and downs of that assignment, but surely there's more to that story.

In addition to siblings and ministry partners, their relationship certainly could be described as an intimate one involving love, trust, and loyalty. While the Bible never uses the term friendship to describe their relationship, the imprint of it is unmistakable. Three episodes especially bring this to light. The first, found in Numbers 12, displays one of the most painful but prevalent aspects of friendship: betrayal. Aaron and their sister Miriam begin to grumble about Moses behind his back. The catalyst for their complaint was his marriage to a Cushite woman, but the specifics don't really matter. While Moses does not hear their gossip, God does. He responds with confrontation, judgment, and punishment. Then Moses responds by pleading with God on their behalf for mercy. We all know how that moment stings; it's an unfortunate price of friendship among sinners.

---

9. Leviticus 11:1; 13:1; 14:33; 15:1.

The second scene demonstrates the strength of their relationship and involves shared suffering. It is recorded in Numbers 16 and 17. Without delving into the particulars of the event too much, which is often referred to as 'Korah's Rebellion,' a few men charged Moses with 'going too far' in setting Aaron up as the head of the priesthood. Hurt and angered by the accusation, Moses leads the people to turn to God for either confirmation of his and Aaron's leadership or of a new direction. In response, God brings judgment on Korah, his co-conspirators, and more than 14,000 Israelites, and He reaffirms Aaron's priestly leadership. Accused by a few and opposed by the congregation, they stand together and persevere in trial.

The third story comes in the chapter that records Aaron's death. Near the end of both their lives, we read of an incident that mirrors one in their first days out of Egypt in Numbers 20. The people quarrel with Moses because they are thirsty and even call into question the goodness and loyalty of God. Moses and Aaron turn to the Lord in prayer, and He gives directions through which He will provide water for the people from a rock. In frustration that every leader and parent understands, Moses fails to follow God's instructions. While Moses responds with impulsive anger, surely they shared the moment of frustration.

As in Eden, friendship is present in the exodus even if it is not named. The lives of these two men were inseparably intertwined in what could be described, like Adam and Eve, as more but not less than friendship. Despite moments of conflict between them, they strengthened and supported one another for four decades of life and ministry. In addition, we begin to observe in this example the way Spirit-empowered friendship enables pastors and those under their care to flourish.

## David and Jonathan

If we surveyed 100 churchgoers and asked them to give an example of friendship in the Old Testament (Family Feud style), I'd expect the number one answer on the board would be this pair. As much as we know about the intimate relationship of love, trust, and loyalty that Jonathan and David shared, it's worth noting at the outset that theirs was an unlikely friendship with monumental hurdles from the first day.

Let's start with Jonathan. He bursts on the scene in 1 Samuel 14 as the deserving and obvious heir apparent to his father, King Saul. For starters, as Saul begins showing signs of failure, Jonathan emerges as a brave, capable warrior and leader. After Jonathan defeats a garrison of Philistines at Geba, Saul gathers the troops at Gilgal. With Israel badly outnumbered, Saul impatiently offered a premature sacrifice which causes Samuel to rebuke him and leave the army. Without the prophet's presence, the army shrinks even smaller in the face of the Philistine threat. Disaster seems unavoidable.

But hope is not lost. Jonathan, with only his armor bearer at his side, engages the Philistines near Michmash and gains the upper hand. That's two Israelites against 36,000 Philistines, and the larger army is thrown into a panic. As they begin to flee, Israel's army hears the chaos and joins in; together they rout the enemy. As his father had done,[10] Jonathan emerges as a judge-like figure. He was raised up by God in the midst of a desperate situation to bring a great victory and deliver His people. In this and the narrative that follows, Jonathan proves a better alternative than his father in every way. Swift succession seems to be in order. But before they pass the mantle of leadership, Saul stumbles again. His failure to carry out God's command leads not only to the rejection of him as king, but to the rejection of his descendants, too. Because of his father's failure, Jonathan will never assume the throne.

Enter David. We know him by looking back through the lens of his place in the history of Israel and the line of Christ. But well before the covenant promises of 2 Samuel 7, David is Jesse's overlooked, youngest son. With so much material on David, we'll try to see his ascent from Jonathan's perspective. A somewhat random connection brings the young David into Saul's court as a part-time musician. He then shows up as a courier to his brothers at the Valley of Elah only to stand up to fight the Philistine giant, Goliath. The victory brings him respect and notoriety in Israel and a place in the king's house by virtue of Saul's promise to give the victor over Goliath to his daughter in marriage.

While we're never told he has any, Jonathan's aspirations for kingship are voided. He had the most natural claim to the throne by both birthright and proven record of leadership, but in walks David with

---

10. 1 Samuel 11.

a giant's head and immediately captures the hearts of the people. As such, Jonathan had every reason to be suspicious, jealous, and even antagonistic toward David. But he isn't. In addition, and based on the sparse timeline we can piece together from the text, it's safe to assume that David is much younger than Jonathan. Despite these obstacles, he embraces David as a friend and loves him from the very beginning.[11]

In 1 Samuel 18:1-15, their relationship is described from Jonathan's perspective in four ways. First, their souls were knitted together as one. More literally, Jonathan attached himself to David with inseparable devotion. Second, he loved David as himself. This word clearly communicates the affection of friendship, and it also likely carries the connotation of political loyalty. Third, Jonathan formalized the devotion of his friendship through a covenant. This binding commitment of loyalty was grounded in love and unity with one another. This language is used most often in the Old Testament to speak of God's relationship to Israel but was commonly used in the Ancient Near East of men who solidified their friendship by making a pact. Thus, Jonathan binds himself to David with commitment to his well-being and success, and they become joined together as brothers.[12] Fourth, Jonathan gives his garments and military weaponry to David. Giving his robe, armor, sword, bow, and belt was not only practically beneficial for David as a warrior, it was

---

11. Despite some modern attempts to describe this relationship as homosexual, the Bible gives no indication of it. In fact, there is not a shred of textual or historical evidence for this claim, and efforts to read it into the story are driven by the modern impulses to subvert the Bible's sexual ethic.

12. 2 Samuel 1:26.

symbolic. These gifts were an acknowledgment of David as the lead warrior in Israel's army and possibly even a hint of recognition that he was now the successor to the throne.

These actions demonstrated extraordinary humility and deference and were the ground for the intimate relationship of love, trust, and loyalty between these two men. Humanly speaking, it is a surprising friendship on a number of levels and proof of Jonathan's character and his faith in the Lord. As David's military success continues, Saul grows jealous while Jonathan remains committed to his friend. In fact, Jonathan displays his love and loyalty in protecting David from his father on more than one occasion. The first recorded incident is in 1 Samuel 19 when Saul directs Jonathan and his servants to kill David. After warning David of the danger, Jonathan convinces Saul not to pursue violence and brings temporary peace between them.

The more well-known story is recorded in the next chapter. This time David learns of Saul's renewed animosity for him and reports it to Jonathan. Unaware of the threat to his friend, Jonathan pledges to investigate and reaffirms his covenant loyalty. Using a clever plan to draw out his father's true intentions, Jonathan discovers the truth. When Saul realizes Jonathan's efforts to protect David, he lashes out at him confirming the cost of Jonathan's loyalty to David by saying, 'as long as the son of Jesse lives on the earth, neither you nor your kingdom shall be established.'[13] Undeterred, Jonathan warns David, they share a tearful goodbye that includes

---

13. 1 Samuel 20:31.

yet another pledge of loyalty to one another, and David flees as a fugitive.

The final reference to their friendship is a brief mention in 1 Samuel 23. David is still on the run from Saul and surrounded by a small band of devoted and capable warriors. Aware of the situation and in an act of care for his friend, Jonathan goes to David. On the heels of being betrayed at Keilah, David was constantly pursued leading him to move frequently, stay in more remote places, and find easily defensible locations. Engulfed in loneliness, discouragement, and fear, the visit from his friend must have brought relief, comfort, and joy.

More than just his presence, Jonathan has a four-fold message for David. First, do not fear. This word speaks to Jonathan's heart and to David's state of mind. Second, he assured David of God's protection. Third, he reiterated God's promise to make David the king. While we have assumed Jonathan's awareness of this fact since the defeat of Goliath, this is the first direct reference to it. He expressed absolute confidence in David's future because he knows God has already decided it. Even more, he's willing to submit to it. Fourth, Jonathan expressed excitement about this plan and commitment to it. Far from jealousy or animosity about being passed over by God as the next king, Jonathan enthusiastically pledges his support. For the third time, we're told that they make a covenant or a mutual pact of love and loyalty before the Lord.

Without doubt, these two men shared God-honoring, spiritual friendship. This final meeting reveals what was evident all along; namely, the characteristics of love, trust, and loyalty. In addition, they demonstrate that Spirit-empowered friendship enables leaders—political, military, and especially spiritual leaders—to flourish along with those under their care.

## Paul and Barnabas

The old Western movie image of the cowboy riding off into the sunset captures a sentiment most of us share. We want our hero to rise above all the challenges, defeat the villain, and retire peacefully on his own terms. But that kind of art rarely imitates real life. Instead, our heroes, who are merely human like us, can't keep it together and the ending almost always leaves something to be desired. Our final portrait of friendship includes one of the more disappointing turns in the story of the early church.

Paul compiled quite the highlight reel. Of course, the missionary, church planter, and writer would deflect the attention and praise knowing it was owing to God's power in Christ working in him through the Spirit. Yet, in the history of the church, few can match the zeal, effectiveness, or impact of his twenty years in public ministry. Born with social and religious pedigree, he received a top-notch education in Jewish law and was set for a respectable career as a religious leader. Even the controversy swirling around the new sect of Jews claiming the Messiah had come only served to his advantage as he emerged as a lead persecutor of them. All that changed when he met this Messiah on a mission to oppress and harm them. In the decade that followed, he learned and ministered more quietly, and we know only the basic details of this period. But that changed with an invitation from a man nicknamed Barnabas.

The two men had crossed paths at least once prior, years earlier in Jerusalem. Before we turn to that story, Barnabas' background is impressive and important as well. The first four chapters in Acts are, pound for pound as they say, about the most exciting in the Bible. They include a commissioning from the risen Lord, a conversation with a couple of angels, prayer meetings, the outpouring of God's Spirit, apostolic preaching, thousands of conversions, courageous witness, miraculous healing, and dramatic confrontations with the religious establishment. That new community demonstrated remarkable faith in God and commitment to one another. At the end of Acts 4, Barnabas is presented as an example of the type of person in that initial group. He emerged as a respected member because of his gift of encouragement and his sacrificial commitment to the community.

Because Paul's reputation as a Jewish leader and persecutor preceded him, the apostles were skeptical of his conversion and therefore slow to welcome him. Barnabas steps in to facilitate a first meeting between them foreshadowing a future ministry partnership. The men go in different directions for the next several years as Paul ministers in Syria and Cilicia while Barnabas remains a staple of the Jerusalem church. They are eventually reunited when Barnabas recruits Paul to join him in Antioch. This ministry flourishes for a year before they are sent as emissaries to Jerusalem to bring famine relief on behalf of the church. They return to Antioch with John (or as he is more commonly known, Mark) and are commissioned a short time later as a missionary team heading west with the gospel. Interestingly, in the references to this tandem through Acts 11 and 12, Barnabas is always listed first.

Acts 13 and 14 recount familiar details of what has come to be known as Paul's first missionary journey. They sail out into the Mediterranean Sea to Cyprus then to Asia Minor. Before working their way by land through Perga to Antioch in Pisidia, Iconium, Lystra, and Derbe, the team shrinks by one member as Mark returns to Jerusalem. They double back through each town in Asia Minor before returning to Antioch. We see evidence of a shifting ministry dynamic between the men from the start of Acts 13 in that Paul is now listed first when they are named. Regardless of the order, these men shared more than a ministry partnership. No doubt, theirs was a relationship of love, trust, and loyalty.

Following this trip, they are confronted with a brewing controversy about the nature of salvation, specifically related to Gentiles. The weeds of that debate are not germane for this book, but thankfully the early Church settled the matter well faithfully, and our missionary team returns to Antioch. Their partnership comes to a sad end as they prepare to launch out on the missionary trail again. The well-known dispute stems from Barnabas' desire to take Mark, who we learn from Colossians was his relative, and Paul's refusal because of Mark's prior act of desertion. We are not told why he left during the first journey, but speculation includes homesickness, fear, physical illness, and theological dispute. In truth, it does not matter. The result is heartbreaking regardless of the reasons.

What a dramatic moment in the life of that church! Two of their most trusted leaders and their all-star missionary team can't settle their dispute and move on together. Their relationship stretched back more than a decade and their ministry partnership for about half of that time. Yet, it comes to an end after only one journey to the mission frontier.

We are tempted to assign blame. Paul was so black and white. He had no grace for poor Mark. He made one mistake and Paul wouldn't let him live it down. Why couldn't he forgive and give him a second chance? It was obviously Paul's fault! On the other hand, Barnabas was blinded by his blood relation to Mark. His trip home was not only dangerous; it jeopardized the team's effectiveness. Perhaps by taking a spot on the current team he was eliminating someone else as an assistant who had proven more reliable. Instead of allowing wisdom to drive him, he was acting out of blind love and loyalty, potentially putting the team at risk. It was obviously Barnabas' fault! But why didn't Mark step up and end the controversy? He could have removed his name from consideration and not allowed the fracture in Paul's and Barnabas' relationship. It was obviously Mark's fault! Still others read more into the fracture by seeing Paul's emergence as the leader as part of the problem.

My favorite part of this passage is that Luke neither hides the issue nor assigns blame. His goal is not to present human heroes, so he has no interest in masking weaknesses or struggles. Furthermore, he doesn't take a side even to defend his Paul, with whom he would travel on subsequent missionary journeys. While the split is necessary for explaining Barnabas' absence during the rest of Acts, it appears the disagreement didn't dissolve their relationship entirely. In fact, Paul writes of Mark's value in 2 Timothy 4, and he affirms Barnabas as an apostle in 1 Corinthians 9, which he wrote years later.

Whatever loss they suffered in proximity appears not to have eliminated their affection and respect for one another. This portrait adds nuance to our understanding of friendship in both its positive and negative aspects. Positively, they display love, trust, and loyalty in numerous ways. Negatively, they show the reality that the vast majority of friendships change over time. Even without major fissures, it's rare for lifelong friends to maintain a consistent level of intimacy owing to distance, changes in stage of life, and even conflict. Regardless, their friendship stands as a powerful example of the type of relationship that God uses to sustain pastors and church leaders. To this end, Luke's record of Paul's continued ministry proves that the void created by this parting was filled by other men, including especially Silas. Despite Barnabas' departure from the story, friendship for Paul remains a constant.

## Conclusion

Friendship is a gift from God to mankind to meet a need that He implanted into our nature. He did not make us for isolation; instead, we are built with an aversion to aloneness. While true for every single person, the Scriptures demonstrate the value of relationships for those who are actively engaged in ministry leadership. Once again, Spirit-empowered friendship is an instrument of God's grace to enable pastors and those under their care to flourish. As these four portraits demonstrate, friendship is a vital tool to help leaders persevere. To this end, modern-day pastors need the gift of intimate relationships of love, trust, and loyalty.

# 2

# A PASTORAL FRIENDSHIP (1)

## BASIL OF CAESAREA AND EUSEBIUS OF SAMOSATA (4TH CENTURY)

Sometimes, the towering giants of church history can feel as close to us as a star in a neighboring galaxy. They're out there somewhere in the distance and an extraordinary sight to behold with proper magnification equipment, but they have virtually nothing to do with our actual lives. For a majority of normal, terrestrial-type pastors, we fear the heroes of history feel as distant as their stories are encouraging. But that's entirely the wrong perspective. Even the most well-known men were Holy-Spirit-empowered clay pots who needed God's grace every bit as much as we do. In fact, the evidence of their dependence on friendship is proof of their frailty and humanity. In this first of two chapters focusing on church history we offer an example of pastoral friendship involving two noteworthy men.

In the fourth century, a number of key Christian authors, like Basil of Caesarea (c. 330–379), Gregory of Nazianzus (c. 329–389), John Chrysostom (347–407), and especially Augustine (354–430), began to write extensively about the subject of friendship.[1] For instance, Gregory Nazianzus, who was for a brief period of time from 379–381 the bishop of Constantinople, highlighted the importance of friendship when he stated: 'If anyone were to ask me, "What is the best thing in life?," I would answer, "Friends".'[2] Chrysostom, in a sermon that he preached in Constantinople around 402 on 1 Thessalonians 2, similarly affirmed the necessity of friendship: 'It were better for us that the sun should be extinguished, than to be deprived of friends; better to live in darkness, than to be without friends. ... I speak of spiritual friends, who prefer nothing to friendship.'[3] To have true, spiritual friends, though, is something of a rarity, according to Chrysostom. In his words:

> If I were speaking of any plant growing in India, of which no one had ever had any experience, no speech would avail to represent it, though I should utter ten thousand words. So also now whatever things I say [about friendship], I say in vain, for no one will be able to understand me. This is a plant that is planted in heaven, having for its branches not heavy-clustered pearls, but a virtuous life, which is far superior. ... The pleasure of friendship excels all others, even if you compare it with the sweetness of honey. For that satiates, but a friend never does, so long as he is a friend; nay, the desire of

1. Carolinne White, *Christian Friendship in the Fourth Century* (Cambridge: Cambridge University Press, 1992).

2. Cited White, *Christian Friendship in the Fourth Century*, p. 70.

3. John Chrysostom, Homily 2 on *1 Thessalonians* (Patrologia Graeca 42.404), trans. John A. Broadus in Philip Schaff, ed., *Nicene and Post-Nicene Fathers, First Series* (Buffalo, NY: Christian Literature Publishing Co., 1889), revised Kevin Knight (https://www.newadvent.org/fathers/230402.htm), altered.

him rather increases, and such pleasure never admits of satiety. Indeed, a friend is sweeter than the present life.[4]

In this chapter, we look at one early Christian friendship in particular, that of Basil of Caesarea in Cappadocia with Eusebius of Samosata (310/330–380). Nineteen extant letters of Basil to Eusebius reveal the extent to which the Cappadocian pastor-theologian came to rely upon Eusebius first as a spiritual mentor, then confidant and companion in prayer. In seeking to understand their friendship, Basil clearly drew upon such biblical patterns of friendship as that of Paul and Timothy, which, like that of Eusebius and Basil, began with an older man mentoring a younger but developed into a friendship of equals. In a time of theological controversy and ecclesial confusion, Basil found enormous help in the letters and prayers of Eusebius.

## The End of Basil's Friendship with Eustathius of Sebaste

By 376 Basil of Caesarea's (c. 329–379) long-standing friendship with another friend, his mentor Eustathius, bishop of Sebaste (c. 300–c. 377), had completely disintegrated.[5] His relationship with Eustathius had been one

---

4. Chrysostom, Homily 2 on *1 Thessalonians* (Patrologia Graeca 42.405–406), trans. Broadus, revised Knight (https://www.newadvent.org/fathers/230402. htm), altered. I have compared this translation with the Greek and adapted it in a few places, following White, *Christian Friendship in the Fourth Century*, p. 92.

5. For Basil's life and thought, see especially Paul Jonathan Fedwick, *The Church and the Charisma of Leadership in Basil of Caesarea* (1979 ed.; repr. Eugene, OR: Wipf and Stock, n.d.); Andrew Radde-Gallwitz, *Basil of Caesarea: A Guide to His Life and Doctrine* (Eugene, OR: Cascade Books, 2012).

of the most significant friendships of his life and stretched back twenty years to the time of Basil's conversion in the mid-350s. At the very beginning of his Christian life, Basil had purposely sought out men whose lives were marked by godliness and whom he could regard, in his own words, as 'fathers and guides of my soul on the journey to God.'[6] Eustathius was initially such a man, but by the late 360s and early 370s it became apparent to Basil that there were such large differences between them when it came to Trinitarian doctrine that their friendship could not progress any further.

Eustathius was largely unconcerned about questions of dogma such as the nature and status of the Holy Spirit, and it was undoubtedly because he was not a theologian that none of his writings have been transmitted. Eustathius appears to have been quite happy to affirm the original Nicene Creed, which essentially said nothing about the Holy Spirit beyond 'We believe in the Holy Spirit.' Eustathius had a deep aversion to expanding it to include a dogmatic assertion with regard to the Spirit. He was committed essentially to

---

On Eustathius and his pneumatology, see especially Michael A.G. Haykin, *The Spirit of God: The Exegesis of 1 and 2 Corinthians in the Pneumatomachian Controversy of the Fourth Century* (Leiden: E. J. Brill, 1994), p. 27, n. 86. On Eustathios' career, see also C.A. Frazee, 'Anatolian Asceticism in the Fourth Century: Eustathios of Sebastea and Basil of Caesarea,' The Catholic Historical Review 66 (1980): pp. 16–33; J. Gribomont, 'Eustathius of Sebaste' in *Encyclopedia of Ancient Christianity,* ed. Angelo Di Berardino et al. (Downers Grove, IL: IVP Academic, 2014), vol. 1, p. 882.

6. Letter 204.6. All translations of Basil's works are by the author unless otherwise indicated. The Greek text used has been that of the four volumes of Roy J. Deferrari, *Saint Basil: The Letters* (Loeb Classical Library; Cambridge, MA: Harvard University Press/London: William Heinemann, 1926–1934).

a Binitarianism that was hostile to any conglorification of the Spirit with the Father and the Son. His refusal to take a clear stance on the Spirit's deity is well captured by a remark he reputedly uttered at a synod in 364 when the question of the Spirit's ontological status was raised: 'I neither choose to name the Holy Spirit God nor dare to call Him a creature.'[7]

Basil retained his friendship with Eustathius, though, in part with the hope of bringing his old friend around to a robust confession of the Spirit's deity. Basil's irenicism, though, made his own orthodoxy suspect to some. In late 372 and early 373, Theodotus of Nicopolis (d. 375), a leading bishop in northern Asia Minor, began to pressure Basil to clarify his own position on the Spirit as well as his relationship with Eustathius. Meletius of Antioch (d. 381), another key supporter of the Nicene Creed, shared Theodotus' view.[8] Basil, by associating with a suspected heretic, was himself dogmatically suspect! Basil found himself in an unenviable position. On the one hand, he was beginning to be criticized by a circle of Eustathius' followers for doctrinal convictions regarding the Spirit that were increasingly unacceptable to many of Eustathius' theological partisans. On the other hand, his close ties to Eustathius were making him dogmatically suspect to a number of his episcopal colleagues and some of his monastic friends.[9]

During the summer of 373 Basil began to pressure Eustathius to commit himself to a more robust Trini-

---

7. Socrates, *Church History* 2.45.

8. For Meletius' theological views, see Haykin, *Spirit of God*, pp. 33–7.

9. Haykin, *Spirit of God*, pp. 31–6.

tarianism. After two meetings Basil was actually sanguine about Eustathius' theological orientation. As he told Eusebius of Samosata, who, as shall be seen, would replace Eustathius in the 370s as Basil's chief mentor and friend: 'we found, with God's help, that he was sincerely following the entirety of the orthodox faith.'[10] At the second of these meetings, in August of 373, Eustathius signed a statement of faith in which he affirmed:

> [We] must anathematize all who call the Holy Spirit a creature, and all who so think; all who do not confess that he is holy by nature, as the Father is holy by nature and the Son is holy by nature, and refuse him his place in the blessed divine nature. Our not separating him from Father and Son is a proof of our right of mind. For we are bound to be baptized in the terms we have received and to profess belief in the terms in which we are baptized, and as we have professed belief in, so to give glory to Father, Son and Holy Spirit.[11]

That fall, though, when Eustathius was to ratify this statement of faith at a meeting with Theodotus and Meletius, he failed to show. Instead, he renounced his signature on the statement and, at a series of Pneumatomachian synods, denounced what he described as the doctrinal innovations of Basil and openly slandered him as a Sabellian.[12] Basil was so stunned by this turn of

---

10. Basil, *Letter* 98.

11. Basil, *Letter* 125.3.

12. For details, see Haykin, *Spirit of God,* pp. 38-9.

events and the betrayal by one of his closest friends that, in his words, 'my heart was crushed.'[13]

During this difficult time, it was another friendship, namely that with Eusebius of Samosata, that was a source of theological strength and spiritual encouragement for the bishop of Caesarea during the most difficult, though extremely fruitful, period of his life.[14]

## Basil's Friendship with Eusebius of Samosata

Given the fact that by 361 Eusebius was already regarded as 'a bishop of great moral authority,'[15] his birth should be placed probably in the first two decades of the fourth century.[16] He became the bishop of Samosata, a city of military and political significance on the upper Euphrates River about 150 miles north-east of Antioch on the Orontes, probably in the 350s. The first extant letter of Basil

---

13. Basil, *Letter* 244.4.

14. The key ancient sources for Eusebius' life are Theodoret, *Church History* 2.27–28; 4.12–13; 5.4; and Sozomen, *Church History* 6.4. For more recent studies, see Henry Robert Reynolds, 'Eusebius (77), bishop of Samosata' in *A Dictionary of Christian Biography and Literature*, ed. Henry Wace and William Piercy (London: John Murray, 1911), pp. 342-3; Markus Vinzent, 'Eusebius of Samosata (Saint)' in *Religion Past & Present: Encyclopedia of Theology and Religion*, ed. Hans Dieter Betz et al. (Leiden: Brill, 2008), 4:667; J. Gribomont, 'Eusebius of Samosata' in *Encyclopedia of Ancient Christianity*, ed. Di Berardino, 1:880.

15. Gribomont, 'Eusebius of Samosata,' p. 880. In Letter 98, dated summer 373, Basil refers to Eusebius' 'venerable age.'

16. Gribomont, 'Eusebius of Samosata,' p. 880. In the words of Raymond Van Dam, Eusebius 'belonged to the generation of Basil's father' (*Families and Friends in Late Roman Cappadocia* [Philadelphia, PA: University of Pennsylvania Press, 2003], p. 35).

to Eusebius was written in either the latter months of 368 or shortly after the advent of 369 and in a lapidary conclusion Basil identified the bishop of Samosata as a spiritual mentor. Basil told Eusebius that he longed to be filled with the 'great treasures of wisdom' that his correspondent possessed.[17] Presumably the two men had met one another personally before this letter. When Basil was ordained bishop of Caesarea in the fall of 370, Eusebius made the journey from Samosata to take part in the episcopal election. Gregory of Nazianzus, who had strongly urged Eusebius to attend, recalled Eusebius' presence as one that filled the hearts of the congregation at Caesarea with 'courage and joy.'[18] Basil would also have been deeply encouraged that such a 'noble guardian of the Faith and watchful ruler of the churches,' as he once called Eusebius, made the arduous journey to lend his support to Basil.[19] Basil wrote again to Eusebius a few months after this ordination, either in December 370 or January of the following year. In this letter he informed Eusebius that he was not only looking forward to the coming of spring after two months of heavy snowfalls that had kept the Cappadocians indoors for much of the time, but was hopeful that Eusebius could revisit Caesarea so that he and his church might 'gain new strength through his good teaching.'[20]

---

17. Basil, *Letter* 27.

18. Gregory of Nazianzus, *Letters* 42 and 44.

19. Basil, *Letter* 136.

20. Basil, *Letter* 48.

In two further letters from the summer of 373, Basil addressed Eusebius as the 'most God-beloved Father,' another indication that Basil considered Eusebius to be his spiritual mentor.[21] That summer or autumn Basil again wrote to Eusebius and told him that he was eager to meet with him so as to 'consult about many things and learn many things.' In fact, Basil continued, he knew of no one like Eusebius who had 'such perfect wisdom and experience garnered from many labours for the churches.'[22] The following year, Basil again commended Eusebius, this time for his foresight and zeal for the spiritual health of the churches in their part of the Empire, 'writing letters, visiting them in person, leaving no act undone, no word unspoken.'[23]

Although they were rare, Basil clearly treasured his actual face-to-face meetings with Eusebius.[24] And yet, he was also thankful that when they could not meet, they could still speak to one another through the medium of the letter. There were times when Basil felt that their letters to one another were like shadows compared to the reality of actually meeting.[25] Nonetheless, when one of Eusebius' letters arrived at a particularly difficult juncture in Basil's life, he compared its effect upon him to the way sailors must feel when, in rough seas, they see 'a beacon fire kindled from afar' on dry land.[26]

---

21. Basil, *Letter* 98.2; 128.2.

22. Basil, *Letter* 138.2.

23. Basil, *Letter* 136.2.

24. See references to such in Basil, *Letter* 27, 34, 48, 95, 127, 136, 138, 145, and 162. See also Basil's letter to Eusebius' nephew, Antiochus, *Letter* 146.

25. Basil, *Letter* 162.

26. Basil, *Letter* 100.

During the pneumatological debates of the 370s that saw the total collapse of his friendship with Eustathius, Basil came to rely deeply upon Eusebius as both mentor and friend. Raymond Van Dam has rightly noted that during this decade the two men came to share 'a deep emotional bond.'[27] A powerful illustration of this bond is seen in a letter that Basil wrote to Eusebius in the early 370s. When one of Basil's other friends, Silvanus, who was bishop of Tarsus, died in 369, there appeared in this city certain individuals who maintained that the Spirit belongs to the creaturely realm. Basil turned to Eusebius for advice and wisdom to deal with the situation as it was threatening to blow the whole church there apart.[28] Now, Basil had a number of ongoing medical conditions, which he frequently mentioned in his letters to Eusebius,[29] and as such he had a multitude of medical illustrations at hand that he employed in various ways in his letters. In this letter Basil likened relief from the distress caused by the pneumatological quarrel in the Tarsus church to anesthetic drugs given by doctors to patients suffering intolerable pain. Where was he to find similar relief from the spiritual distress caused by the quarrels at Tarsus? Basil suggested two sources—first, prayer and then, contemplation of the person of Eusebius. With regard to the latter he wrote:

---

27. Van Dam, *Families and Friends,* p. 36.

28. Basil, Letter 34. For details regarding the theological crisis in Tarsus at this time, see Basil, *Letters* 113–4. Also see Michael A.G. Haykin, 'And Who is the Spirit? Basil of Caesarea's Letters to the Church at Tarsus,' Vigiliae Christianae 41 (1987), 377-85.

29. In the following letters to Eusebius, for example, Basil related to his friend details of his various illnesses: *Letter* 30, 34, 100, 136, 138, 141, 145, 162, 198, 237.

Though we are indeed distressed, we experience this consolation: that we can contemplate your kindness and alleviate the soul's distress by thinking of you and remembering you. For just as the eyes, after looking intently at glistening objects, obtain some relief by turning back to blues and greens, so also, to our souls, the memory of your gentleness and gracefulness is like a gentle touch that wipes away the pain. ... May the Lord graciously grant you to us and to his churches for the benefit of our life and correction of our souls, and may he count me worthy of another beneficial meeting with you.[30]

Basil's language here is yet further evidence of the fact that he clearly regarded Eusebius as a spiritual mentor, one whose wisdom would not only benefit the Church but also Basil personally. Basil used a chromatic illustration to drive home to Eusebius the benefit he had derived from him. After one's eyes have looked at a brilliant object—and here Basil probably had in mind the sun—it was difficult to focus, and it was a relief to look at the blue sea and green vegetation of this world. Similarly, Basil found relief from preoccupation with the problems of the Tarsus church by thinking about the kindness of Eusebius.

During their correspondence Basil frequently mentioned his need for and appreciation of Eusebius' prayers.[31] For example, in the autumn of 373, Basil sought Eusebius' advice regarding three specific issues: how best to respond to certain Western bishops regarding the resolution of a schism

---

30. Basil, *Letter* 34.

31. See, for example, Basil, *Letter* 27, 30, 100, 141, 162, and 239.1.

in Antioch, how to help those in Sebaste who had rejected what Basil called the 'festering ulcer of Eustathius' wicked doctrine,' and how to fulfill a request for Basil to appoint a bishop in the city of Iconium though the city lay outside of his diocese.[32] Illness prevented Basil from meeting with Eusebius in person, and thus he asked his mentor to send him written answers to the three queries. But if he did not have time to do that, then Basil wanted him to pray:

> Pray that what is pleasing to the Lord may come into my mind. And in your synod request that we be remembered, and pray for us yourself, and also include the people as you pray, that we might be counted worthy to serve so as to please the Lord in the days and hours of our pilgrimage that remain.[33]

One of Basil's last extant letters to Eusebius was written two years later in the fall of 375. In the previous year the Homoean Emperor Valens (328–378) had removed a number of Nicene bishops from their charges, among them Eusebius, who had been banished to Thrace.[34] Eusebius could no longer shepherd his people in person but, in Basil's words, he could still engage in 'earnest prayer on behalf of the churches,' even as Moses had prayed unceasingly during Israel's battle with the Amalekites.[35] This comparison with Moses was among the highest compliments that Basil could give to Eusebius, for Basil

---

32. Basil, *Letter* 138.2.

33. Basil, *Letter* 138.2.

34. Theodoret, *Church History vol. 4*, pp. 12-13.

35. Basil, *Letter* 241.

regarded the Israelite leader as 'a paragon of self-sacrificial love, contemplation, [and] nearness to God.'[36]

## Conclusion

After the break with Eustathius of Sebaste in the mid-370s, Basil found himself compelled to write his masterly work on the deity of the Holy Spirit, *On the Holy Spirit*, which is the first theological treatise dedicated to the person of the Holy Spirit. It is a milestone work in the history of Christian doctrine. This is all well known. What is not well known, though, is that sustaining and helping Basil through this time was his friendship with Eusebius of Samosata, a Moses-like prayer-warrior and mentor to Basil. We'll grant that few in any generation will write a treatise that persists in influence 1,600 years from now, but every pastor of every generation will need a Moses-like prayer-warrior and friend. Learn from Basil and invest your energy in cultivating friendship.

---

36. Andrea Sterk, *Renouncing the World Yet Leading the Church: The Monk-Bishop in Late Antiquity* (Cambridge, MA; London, England: Harvard University Press, 2004), p. 62.

# 3

# A PASTORAL FRIENDSHIP (2)

## BENJAMIN FRANCIS AND JOSHUA THOMAS
## (18TH CENTURY)

We love Romans 16. Of course, we love every chapter of the Bible, but it may sound odd because it seems less significant among the mountain peaks of Paul's letter to the church at Rome. The beauty of it lies, at least in part, in the obscurity of the people mentioned. In his attempt to build rapport and bolster his credibility, he mentions more people by name than in any other New Testament letter. Save a few who appear prominently elsewhere, the names on his list are mostly forgotten figures in the annals of church history. They may be obscure to us, but in God's eyes they were significant to God's kingdom in their place and time. Church history is replete with gems to encourage and inspire us, especially when it comes to pastoral friendship. From the annals of anonymity, we offer Benjamin Francis and Joshua Thomas.

In the English speaking world of the eighteenth century, there appears to have been an outpouring of noteworthy 'claims for the life-enhancing value of intimate friendship.'[1] And in the words of George Haggerty, 'friendship held a special place in the eighteenth-century imagination.'[2] In many ways, this era—variously called the Age of Reason or the Age of Revival—saw what was tantamount to the emergence of friendship as a central value in Western culture. And pastors were not immune to these cultural forces. For instance, friendship for Samuel Buell (1716–1798), a pastor in East Hampton, Long Island, was 'a divine and spiritual relation of minds, a union of souls, a marriage of hearts, and a harmony of designs and affections; and which is usually productive of happiness beyond expression.'[3] Buell was thus confident that:

> Friendship is one of the most considerable branches of our felicity ... Life without friendship and society, though attended with the utmost affluence of all other outward comforts, in their rich variety, would be a rayless gloom. Perfect solitude would wither all the glories of Eden, and turn it into a desert, and a palace into a dungeon. Paradise itself appeared in part unblessed, till joyous friendship crowned and consummated its blooming pleasures. Friendship is the bond of bliss in the upper world, where all is harmony, all is love; and in this our world, it affords a sort of life-sustaining power, and

---

1. Keith Thomas, *The Ends of Life: Roads to Fulfilment in Early Modern England* (Oxford: Oxford University Press, 2009), pp. 191-3.

2. George Haggerty, 'Horace Walpole's Epistolary Friendships,' *British Journal for Eighteenth-Century Studies* 29 (2006), p. 201.

3. Samuel Buell, *The Divine Agency acknowledged in the Death of our dearest Friends* (New York, NY: J. Parker and W. Weyman, 1757), p. 10, spelling modernized. For this text from Buell and the next one, I am indebted to Scott Bowman.

virtuous balm, for fainting minds, under over-bearing sorrows, and pours the lustre of day into souls over-clouded with afflictive night.[4]

On the other side of the Atlantic, the Baptist poetess Anne Steele (1717–1778) similarly described 'true friendship' as 'the noblest earthly gift/Which heaven on man bestows.' Indeed, Steele affirmed, 'Not mines afford a gem of equal worth.'[5] In this chapter, we look at the way this emphasis on friendship in the eighteenth century impacted two Welsh Baptist pastors, Benjamin Francis (1734–1799) and Joshua Thomas (1719–1797), and how their amity illustrates the truth of Proverbs 27:17: 'As iron sharpens iron, so one person sharpens another' (NIV).

## Benjamin Francis

Benjamin Francis was, in many respects, a remarkable individual. He was the youngest son of Enoch Francis (1688–1740), the most respected Welsh Baptist minister of his day.[6] Orphaned at the age of six, the younger Francis was later convinced that he personally experienced God's

---

4. Buell, *Divine Agency*, p. 5, spelling modernized.

5. Anne Steele, 'On the Same' in her *Poems on Subjects Chiefly Devotional*, New ed. (Bristol: W. Pine, 1780), vol. 1, p. 203.

6. For the life of Francis, the following sources have been extremely helpful: Thomas Flint, 'A Brief Narrative of the Life and Death of the Rev. Benjamin Francis, A.M.,' annexed to John Ryland, Jr., *The Presence of Christ the Source of eternal Bliss. A Funeral Discourse,... occasioned by the Death of the Rev. Benjamin Francis, A.M.* (Bristol, 1800), pp. 33–76; Geoffrey F. Nuttall, 'Questions and Answers: An Eighteenth-Century Correspondence,' *The Baptist Quarterly* 27 (1977–1978),. 83–90; *idem*, 'Letters by Benjamin Francis,' *Trafodion* (1983), 4–8. I have also benefited from Gwyn Davies, 'A Welsh Exile: Benjamin Francis (1734–99)' (Unpublished ms., 1999), 3 pages.

saving grace when he was but a boy. Baptized at Swansea when he was fifteen, Francis began to preach four years later.

His ministry began at a time when far too many English and Welsh Particular (or Calvinistic) Baptist congregations were stymied in their growth by Hyper-Calvinism or insular thinking, or just plain apathy. Francis, though, went on to be trained at Bristol Baptist Academy where a vibrant evangelical Calvinism was not only preserved but also actively fostered.[7] Due in part to this training at Bristol, Francis eventually played a significant role in the renewal and revival that came to the Particular Baptists later in the century. As British Baptist historian Raymond Brown has noted with regard to a number of the students who studied at Bristol:

> Many of...[the] Bristol students brought an outstanding contribution to the life of the churches in the second half of the eighteenth century. Men like John Ash (1724–79) of Pershore, Benjamin Beddome (1717–95) of Bourton-on-the-Water and Benjamin Francis of Horsley were content to serve their respective churches for between forty and fifty years, pouring their entire working ministry into the pastoral care of rural congregations, faithful biblical preaching, the development of association life, the establishment of new causes and, in each case, the composition or publication of hymns. Their devotional hymnology, passion for associating,

---

7. See Roger Hayden, 'Evangelical Calvinism among eighteenth-century British Baptists with particular reference to Bernard Foskett, Hugh and Caleb Evans and the Bristol Baptist Academy, 1690-1791' (Ph.D. thesis, University of Keele, 1991).

and evangelistic initiatives helped to divert many churches from high Calvinism and introduced them to these influences which were powerfully at work in the Evangelical Revival.[8]

Francis studied in Bristol from 1753 to 1756. When he first arrived in Bristol, his knowledge of English was so slight that he could not even return thanks for his food in the language. Bernard Foskett (1685–1758), the Principal of the Academy, was of the opinion that Francis should be sent back to Wales because of the language barrier. However, the younger tutor at the school, Hugh Evans (1713–1781), himself a Welshman and who had been converted under the preaching of Enoch Francis, pleaded that Benjamin be allowed to stay. By dint of study, Francis eventually obtained a thorough knowledge of English so that he could preach with complete ease in either it or Welsh.

After he graduated Francis preached for a while in Chipping Sodbury, Gloucestershire. Eventually, in 1757, he moved to Horsley where, the following year, he was ordained at the age of twenty-four.[9] Although the church there consisted of sixty-six members, most of them were poor artisans and clothworkers and were unable to provide enough financially for his support. Francis once described the circumstances of most of the congregation as being 'extremely indigent.' And near the end of his life, he remarked that his congregation

---

8. Raymond Brown, *The English Baptists of the Eighteenth Century* (London: The Baptist Historical Society, 1986), pp. 84–5.

9. For a brief account of the early history of the Horsley church, see Albion M. Urdank, *Religion and Society in a Cotswold Vale, Nailsworth, Gloucestershire, 1780–1865* (Berkeley, CA: University of California Press, 1990), pp. 90–3.

was for the most part 'poor, plain, and have not had the advantage of literature.'[10] Thus, 'he was obliged to rear pigs, to grow his own fruit and vegetables, to keep a school, and to venture into the woollen trade (with disastrous financial consequences) in order to make ends meet.'[11]

Alongside these monetary problems, Francis also experienced a long series of domestic trials. In 1765, his first wife and three of their children all died within the space of three months. He married again a year later to an Abigail Wallis. They had ten children, of whom they buried seven![12] In the midst of these deeply distressing circumstances Francis drew comfort from the piety that a number of his dying children exhibited. For instance, when one of the children from his second marriage, Hester, was dying at the age of eleven in August 1790, she told her mother: 'My soul is as full of joy as it can contain—the Lord is become my salvation—the gates of heaven are open to me, and I shall soon be there.' Her last words to her father were: 'I love you, but I love Christ more.'[13]

Despite these deep trials, Francis proved to be a tireless evangelist, one, we are told, who delighted in 'telling poor sinners the unsearchable riches of his compassionate Redeemer.'[14] During his time at Horsley, Francis baptized

---

10. Cited in Urdank, *Religion and Society in a Cotswold Vale*, p. 95; Nuttall, 'Letters by Benjamin Francis,' p. 6.

11. Davies, 'Welsh Exile,' p. 2. On Francis' financial problems, see also Flint, 'Brief Narrative,' p. 49.

12. Flint, 'Brief Narrative,' pp. 49–52.

13. Benjamin Francis, 'Obituary: Miss Hester Francis' in John Rippon, ed., The Baptist Annual Register 1 (1790–1793), 158–9.

14. Circular Letter of the Western Association (1800), 2.

nearly 450 persons who had been converted under his ministry. At the time of his death the number of members in his church was 252. The meeting house was enlarged three times during Francis' ministry, so that by the early nineteenth century the church was one of the largest in the English Particular Baptist community. Francis attributed much of the success that attended his preaching to the Sunday prayer meetings the church held at six o'clock in the morning and in the afternoon before the afternoon service. Fifty or sixty came to the Sunday morning prayer meeting, while at the afternoon prayer meeting, the vestry would literally overflow with people.[15]

None of Francis' sermons appear to have survived. Describing his preaching, Flint emphasized that Francis was always concerned 'to declare the whole counsel of God,' even when he preached for other denominational bodies. Firm in expressing his doctrinal convictions, he was also a compassionate preacher, who often openly wept for his hearers.[16] While none of Francis' sermons are extant, we do have some of his poems,[17] including a variety of polemical pieces,[18] and a number of elegies, among them ones for John Gill (1697–1771) and George Whitefield

---

15. 'A List of the Particular Baptist Churches in England, 1798' in John Rippon, ed., The Baptist Annual Register 3 (1798-1801), 14-15.

16. Flint, 'Brief Narrative,' p. 47.

17. See, for example, Benjamin Francis, The Conflagaration (Bristol, 1770) or his The Association in John Rippon, ed., Baptist Annual Register 1 (1790–1793), 17–20.

18. See, for instance, Benjamin Francis, The Socinian Champion or priestleyan divinity (London: T. Bensley, 1788) is a critique of the Unitarianism of Joseph Priestley (1733–1804).

(1714–1770).[19] There is also a two-volume collection of his hymns in Welsh entitled *Aleluia*. Only a few of them, though, have ever been translated into English.[20]

## 'Queries and Solutions'

In the archives of Bristol Baptist College there is an unpublished manuscript that records a precious friendship, that of Benjamin Francis, and a fellow Welshman Joshua Thomas, who for forty-three years was the pastor of the Baptist cause in Leominster.[21] The manuscript is actually a transcript, drawn up by Thomas, of letters that passed between him and Francis from 1758 to 1770.[22]

The practice of Francis and Thomas appears to have been for one of them to mail two or three queries periodically to the other. Then, some months later the recipient mailed back his answers, together with fresh questions of his own. These answers were commented on, the new questions answered and both the comments and answers mailed back along with new queries, and so forth. All in all, there are sixty-eight questions and answers in two

---

19. See Benjamin Francis, *An Elegy on the Death of the Rev. John Gill* (London, 1772); *idem*, *Elegy on George Whitefield* (Bristol, 1771).

20. For a listing of most of Francis' works, see Edward C. Starr, *A Baptist Bibliography* (Rochester, NY: American Baptist Historical Society, 1963), 8:71–3.

21. On Thomas, see Kennedy Hart, 'Joshua Thomas 1719–1797' in Michael A.G. Haykin and Terry Wolever, ed., *The British Particular Baptists* (Springfield, MO: Particular Baptist Press, 2018), 4:274–289.

22. 'Queries and Solutions of Joshua Thomas and Benjamin Francis of Horsley 1758–70, being the answers of one to questions posed by the other on matters of theology, church government, preaching' (MS G.98.5; Bristol Baptist College Library, England), 2 vols.

volumes—fifty-eight in the first volume, the remaining ten in Volume II. On only one occasion during these years from 1758 to 1770 was there a noticeable gap in correspondence. That was in 1765 when Francis lost his wife and his three youngest children.

It is noteworthy that at the beginning of the correspondence the two friends sign their letters simply with their names or initials. However, as time passes, their mutual confidence and intimacy deepens, and they begin to write 'yours endearingly' or 'yours unfeignedly' and even 'yours indefatigably' or 'yours inexpressibly.' It was in October 1762, that Thomas first signed himself 'your cordial Brother Jonathan,' and in the following February Francis replied with 'your most affectionate David.' From this point on this is the way the two friends refer to each other. It is noteworthy that the eighteenth-century world, of which Francis and Thomas were a part, looked upon the friendship of David and Jonathan as the exemplar of true friendship.[23]

The questions and their answers are extremely instructive as to the areas of personal theological interest among mid-eighteenth-century Calvinists. But what we also see in this text is the way that two pastors encouraged one another as iron sharpens iron (Prov. 27:17). For instance, the question is asked, 'When may a Minister conclude that he is influenced and assisted by the Spirit of God in studying and ministering the Word?'[24] Queries are raised about

---

23. Ruth Smith as cited in Haggerty, 'Horace Walpole's Epistolary Friendships,' p. 201.

24. 'Queries and Solutions,' vol i, p. 13. The spelling and capitalization have been modernized in the quotations from this text.

the eternal state of dead infants,[25] how best to understand the remarks in Revelation 20 about the millennium,[26] and about whether or not inoculation against that dreaded killer of the eighteenth century, smallpox, was right or wrong.[27]

A good number of the queries relate to what we would call 'spirituality.' In 1763, for instance, Francis asked Thomas, 'Is private fasting a moral or ceremonial Duty? and consequently is it a duty under the Gospel?'[28] When Thomas sent his response to this question, one of his return queries was, 'What are the best means of revival, when a person is flat and dead in his soul?'[29] Other similar questions include the following: 'How often should a Christian pray?'[30] 'When may a Christian be said to be active and lively in his soul?'[31] 'Wherein doth communion and fellowship with God consist?'[32]

## 'Lord, teach me to pray!'

Let's look closer at those questions and answers that relate to prayer. 'How often should a Christian pray?' To this very vital question posed by Francis, Thomas had an extensive answer. He dealt first with what he called the 'ejaculatory kind' of prayer—prayers that arise spontaneously during

---

25. 'Queries and Solutions,' i, 56–9, 66–7.

26. 'Queries and Solutions,' i, 59.

27. 'Queries and Solutions,' i, 221–2.

28. 'Queries and Solutions,' i, 195.

29. 'Queries and Solutions,' i, 223.

30. 'Queries and Solutions,' i, 199.

31. 'Queries and Solutions,' i, 228 (asked by Francis).

32. 'Queries and Solutions,' i, 243 (asked by Thomas).

the course of a day's activities—and then the prayers offered during times set apart specifically for prayer, what a later generation of Evangelicals would call 'the quiet time.' In response to Thomas' answer, Francis confessed to his friend—whom he called 'my Jonathan':

> I wish all our brethren of the tribe of Levi were so free from lukewarmness, on the one hand, and enthusiasm, formality and superstition on the other, as my Jonathan appears to be. I am too barren in all my prayers, but I think mostly so in closet prayer (except at some seasons) which tempts me in some measure to prefer a more constant ejaculatory prayer above a more statedly closet prayer, though I am persuaded neither should be neglected. Ejaculatory prayer is generally warm, free, and pure, though short: but I find closet prayer to be often cold, stiff or artificial, as it were, and mixed with strange impertinences & wanderings of heart. Lord teach me to pray! O that I could perform the duty always, as a duty and a privilege and not as a task and a burden![33]

In another of Francis' comments we find the same honesty and humility: 'How languid my faith, my hope, my love! how cold and formal am I in secret devotions!'[34] These remarks surely stem from deep-seated convictions about the vital importance of prayer. Francis would undoubtedly have agreed with Thomas' remark that a believer's 'Great and chief delight, his meat and drink, the life of his life' is his closet prayer and communion with God.[35]

---

33. 'Queries and Solutions,' i, 213–4.

34. 'Queries and Solutions,' i, 235.

35. 'Queries and Solutions,' i, 235.

Francis' transparent remarks also have their root in Francis' belief that because the Lord had led him to seek Christ at a very young age—and, in his words, 'overwhelmed me with joy by a sense of his love'—he should have been more eager to pray out of a sense of gratitude. Instead, he confessed, 'A stupid, indolent, sensual or legal temper sadly clog the wings of my prayers.'[36] Thomas sought to encourage Francis by reminding him that 'closet prayer [is like] the smoke on a windy day. When it is very calm the smoke will ascend and resemble an erect pillar, but when windy, as soon as it is out it is scattered to and fro, sometimes 'tis beaten down the chimney again and fills the house. Shall I not thus give over? Satan would have it so, and flesh would have it so, but I should be more earnest in it.'[37]

Francis sought to pray to God twice daily, but he confessed that his difficulties with following a discipline of a set time for prayer stemmed from his being away from his home a lot of the time. He also admitted that he had taken up 'an unhappy habit of sleeping in the morning much longer' than he should have.[38] And this cut into valuable time for prayer. He did not try to excuse such failings. How much has changed since Francis' day—and yet how much remains the same: the same struggle with sin and poor habits that hinder our praying and devotion.

---

36. 'Queries and Solutions,' ii, 63.

37. 'Queries and Solutions,' i, 218.

38. 'Queries and Solutions,' ii, 64.

In 1767 Thomas asked his friend, 'How may one know whether his Prayers are answered or not?'[39] Francis gave six brief reasons:

1.  By the removal of the evil prayed against, or the reception and enjoyment of the good prayed for.

2.  By the peculiar and extraordinary circumstances that may attend the removal of the evil or the reception of the good: as the success of Abraham's servant, etc.

3.  When one does not receive the blessing prayed for, but receives another, perhaps not thought of by him, yet more seasonable, needful and useful.

4.  When he is assisted by the Spirit to pray, to pray in faith, and to wrestle with God. His prayer will then be answered, whether he perceives it or no, or whether he lives to see it or no, yea though he does not receive the particular good he prays for.

5.  When God meets, that is, revives and relieves him in prayer, that is a speedy way in which God answers the prayer of His people. 'I will not remove thy sore affliction, Paul, though thou hast intreated me thrice; but my grace shall be sufficient for thee to bear it.' Thus, God sometimes answers a prayer with a promise, but not the immediate blessing.

6.  In general, one may conclude that God answers his prayers, when he is made more holy and resigned to the will of God, and enabled to persevere in all the duties of religion, and to rejoice in the God of his salvation.[40]

---

39. 'Queries and Solutions', ii, 3.

40. 'Queries and Solutions', ii, 3–4.

The last of these six answers is especially important. It displays the mature realization that four of the most important things for which we could pray are: (1) growth in holiness; (2) unreserved commitment to God's sovereign will over one's life; (3) perseverance; and (4) a heart of joy in God.

When Francis died in 1799, it is noteworthy that what was remembered by his close friends in regard to his devotion were his 'fervent prayers.' What they may not have known was the vital way that Francis' close and intimate friend, Joshua Thomas, had helped Francis persevere as a man of prayer. And so, iron had sharpened iron then, as it continues to do so today.

# PART 2

# LOOKING AHEAD

# 4

# THE COMMAND FOR FRIENDSHIP

The friendships we observed in the past among God's people laid important groundwork by encouraging and warning us. Despite personal flaws, sinful actions, and circumstantial challenges, those friendships proved to be gifts from God and instruments for shaping and sustaining His people. Viewed in light of the biblical directives, they are more than merely historic points of interest. Instead, God uses them to nudge us toward replicating them in relationships characterized by love, trust, and loyalty. More directly, God not only preserved them for us to see; He commands us to develop them ourselves.

No single biblical text proclaims, 'Thou shalt make friends,' but we stand on the authority of God's Word to conclude it is a reasonable application for all who follow Christ. By virtue of their place in front of their congregations, pastors bear special responsibility to lead people toward this end by modeling it for them. We aim in this chapter, therefore, to establish friendship as an expectation for every follower of Jesus—especially for pastors—upon three arguments. First, we show, by implication in the communal nature of God that is reflected in humanity, that friendship is part of God's design for His people. Second, we show, by implication in the relationship between Jesus and the Apostle Peter, that friendship is part of God's design for His people. Third, we show, through the explicit directives about human relationships in general, and about those within the church in particular, that friendship is part of God's design for His people.

## The Implicit Command in God's Communal Nature and its Reflection in Humanity

God is a relational Being. While He has no need for a relationship with mankind, the triune nature of God reveals that connection with another is fundamental to Him. His primary and essential union is with Himself. God is One and God is Three. The eternal 'God reveals Himself to us as Father, Son, and Holy Spirit, with distinct personal attributes, but without division of nature, essence, or being.'[1] While our understanding of God skims the surface, the 'riches and wisdom and knowledge'[2] of what can be known about Him, the communion within the Godhead is unmistakable. God exists in relation to Himself.

The precise nature of this unique relationship among the Persons of the Trinity remains a mystery in many

---

1. Southern Baptist Convention, *Baptist Faith and Message* 2000. https://bfm.sbc.net/bfm2000/#ii-god, Accessed June 21, 2021.

2. Romans 11:33.

regards, but the fact of it is well-attested to in the Scriptures, and particularly in the New Testament Gospels. Critical portions of Jesus' final discourse in John, for example, reveal truth about this relationship.

> But the Helper, the Holy Spirit, whom the Father will send in My name, He will teach you all things, and bring to your remembrance all that I have said to you (John 14:26 NKJV).

> When the Spirit of truth comes, he will guide you into all the truth, for he will not speak on his own authority, but whatever he hears he will speak, and he will declare to you the things that are to come. He will glorify me, for he will take what is mine and declare it to you. All that the Father has is mine; therefore I said that he will take what is mine and declare it to you (John 16:13-15).

Within the mountain of truth and encouragement in these verses is evidence of the distinctions and relationship between the Persons of the Godhead. Based on the broader testimony of Scripture, He always acts in perfect faithfulness, love, and loyalty. So while we avoid using the language of God having a friendship with Himself, the foundation for the concept of friendship emanates from the nature of God and from His relationality.

In addition to His relationship with Himself, which points us broadly in the direction of friendship, God wove this attribute into human beings as displayed by His relating to Adam and Eve. The description of their relationship is somewhat incomplete based on the scant material in Genesis 1–3. However, we see evidence of intimacy, love, trust, and loyalty between the Creator and the first two people. They did not enjoy a precisely reciprocal relationship with God; rather, He moved toward them in grace by stooping to walk with them and allowing them to know and talk with Him. This story demonstrates the nature of God in relating to people and the reflection of that nature in the crown of His creation as they related back to Him.

God's relationality is then reflected through this capacity manifested in humans as they relate to one another. In a way that mirrors Him, people relate to one another. As we touched on in chapter one, this pre-Fall description directs us to the implication that relationships of love, trust, and loyalty are a foundational aspect of God's design of and for humans. We do not enjoy the pre-Fall world, but the consequences of the Fall add to rather than detract from this emphasis on relationships. To begin, enmity with God, which is a central result of sin, could be described as a relational loss. Paul's well-known words express the totality of our loss succinctly, 'For the wages of sin is death.'[3] The most obvious manifestation of this death is physical because it's tangibly measured, but more significant is spiritual death connected to God's wrath. His settled reaction to sin, which is aimed at all who reject His authority and rebel against Him, turns His face against us.[4] The New Testament language of reconciliation highlights this problem from the perspective of God's work to correct it.

God shows his love for us in that while we were still sinners, Christ died for us. Since, therefore, we have

---

3. Romans 6:23.

4. Isaiah 59:2.

now been justified by his blood, much more shall we be saved by him from the wrath of God. For if while we were enemies we were reconciled to God by the death of his Son, much more, now that we are reconciled, shall we be saved by his life (Rom. 5:8-10).

In Christ, God solves all the problems created by our sin, which include the relational fracture between Him and us and the fracture between men. God's heart for reconciliation and His self-sacrificial acts to mend human brokenness reveal His commitment to His glory, first and foremost. But they also express His desire for reunion. He turns back and moves toward us in grace to demolish the dividing wall separating us and to bring us into a right relationship with Him. Or we could say, He befriends us. Thus, stemming from God's relational nature, He establishes a new relationship with people, who are unique among His creation and have the capacity to reciprocate and reflect this attribute, however imperfectly.

This reconciliation with God, then, extends into reconciliation with others. In fact, as noted in 2 Corinthians 5, it is the ground for it. God is our first true friend. Before He befriends us, we have neither the nature nor the power to connect in true love, trust, and loyalty with Him or rightly with anyone else for that matter. This restored relationship with our Creator by grace, through faith in Jesus, makes God-honoring, joy-producing, soul-nourishing friendship with others possible. Without the gospel, some version of friendship is possible, but because we cannot join with others in meaningful, lasting, and spiritually-helpful ways without it, true friendship is impossible. Through the gospel, however, our capacity and capability for friendship is restored as an extension of the renewed relationship with God. This point is further proven by Paul's subsequent admonition in 2 Corinthians 6 concerning our connections with unbelievers. Most translations use the phrase 'unequally yoked' in verse 14 to convey the sense of disconnect between those who have been reconciled to God and those who have not. Often the principle is applied to marriage, but it's much broader. Intimate relationships of love, trust, and loyalty are possible only when both parties have been reconciled to God. Of course, through common grace, God does give unbelievers a taste of this blessing in friendships and marriage, but these relationships never approach God's design without reunion with Him first.

All who have been reconciled to God receive a ministry of reconciliation that calls others to unite with Him and then with others. The communal God communes with us by His grace through His work in Christ, and then He enlivens and empowers our communion with others. Friendships, then, are not merely made possible in Christ; they are assumed or even commanded by implication. Pastors, who lead in this gospel ministry of reconciliation through proclamation, must also lead by modeling restored relationships with God and with others in friendship.

## The Implicit Command through the Example of Jesus

Friendship with Jesus during His earthly ministry was asymmetrical rather than reciprocal. Early drafts of this book's outline included His relationship with Peter as a portrait alongside those in chapter one. Yet, the more we studied the biblical text and the nature of friendship, the distinctions discredited that line of thinking. This example conveys important truth and supports our theme and thrust, but it contributes by exhortation rather than example.

Jesus is the incarnate Son of God; He's the co-equal, co-eternal, fully-divine, only-begotten second Person of the Trinity. Through the incarnation, 'he became flesh and dwelt among us' showing us His glory as the only Son of the Father.[5] While full in His humanity and like us, He remained full in His deity and so He was, at the same time, very much unlike us. Friendship oversimplifies their relationship, but He maintained a perfect and intimate relationship of love, trust, and loyalty with the Father. Jesus also related perfectly to other people. Despite some aspects of mutuality, though, His relationship with mankind had uneven components as well. His friendship to Peter demonstrates it.

Peter's story reads like a roller coaster with exhilarating highs, disheartening lows, stomach-churning turns, and inspiring courage. These moments are woven together to culminate in an ending that could accurately be described as beautiful, sad, and happy. According to the biblical record, he was a hard-working, Jewish man with a small fishing business with his brother, Andrew, who introduced him to Jesus. This first meeting appears to have been as abrupt as it was meaningful. Upon seeing him, Jesus addressed him by his Hebrew name, Simon, and then gave him a new one,

---

5. John 1:14.

Cephas, (or Peter). This brief interaction foreshadows the transformation that is to come.

His calling to leave the fishing business behind and follow Jesus comes a short time later. Jesus took the initiative to beckon Peter, which moved their relationship to a much deeper level. Not yet fully in bloom, but love, trust, and loyalty accurately describe Peter's response of dropping his nets to join Jesus. Most are familiar with the highlights of the next three or so years. Peter became the leader among Jesus' twelve closest disciples[6] and the stories of his successes and failures are known even to most casual readers of the New Testament. A few references capture it well. The first, recorded in Matthew 14:22-33, recounts Peter walking on the Sea of Galilee with Jesus and then sinking because of his faltering faith. Then Mark 8:27-33 recounts Peter's confession of Jesus as the Messiah followed by his attempt to rebuke Jesus. In both stories, before readers have much opportunity to exalt Peter or envy his courage and wisdom, he tumbles back to earth. Of course, the depth of his struggle is epitomized by his three denials of Jesus, which are followed only weeks later, and on the other side of Jesus' resurrection, by his leading the exploding church in Jerusalem with anointed preaching and resolve. In the three decades that follow, he continued as one of the most important leaders in the Church through his public ministries of preaching and writing. The testimony of his leadership is overwhelmingly positive, but not perfect.

---

6. When the Twelve are listed in the New Testament, he is always listed first. See Matthew 10:2, Mark 3:16; Luke 6:14, and Acts 1:13.

The incident of Peter's waffling in Antioch, described by Paul in his letter to the Galatians, yet again demonstrates the humanity that plagued him, and plagues all followers of Christ. Finally, church history testifies to his death as a martyr, which is sad in the way death always is.[7] Yet it provides a beautiful picture of devotion to Christ and points us joyfully toward Him as Lord.

Peter's transformation is undeniable, and it undeniably stems from his relationship to Jesus. He had an intimate relationship of love, trust, and loyalty with Jesus that profoundly changed him and steered his life. And while that was a two-way relationship in some respects, it was mostly unilateral. Jesus was a friend to Peter in ways that Peter never was and never could be to Jesus. To understand this relationship more fully, consider two passages in John's Gospel. The first comes as part of Jesus' teaching on the eve of His crucifixion in John 15:12-17. This paragraph grows from the preceding text in which Jesus used the memorable metaphor of the vine and branches to illustrate the relationship of dependence His disciples have with Him. Through this vital connection to Jesus, we bear the fruit of obedience to and love for Him.

This abiding in Christ also spills over in love for others as is evident in Jesus' straightforward command for His disciples to 'love one another as I have loved you.' Those who know Him intimately will mirror His love. In asserting Himself as a model for them, He describes their relationship using the language of friendship.

---

7. John Foxe, *Foxe's book of Martyrs*, (Newberry, FL: Bridge-Logos, 2001), p. 9.

'This is my commandment, that you love one another as I have loved you. Greater love has no one than this, that someone lay down his life for his friends. You are my friends if you do what I command you. No longer do I call you servants, for the servant does not know what his master is doing; but I have called you friends, for all that I have heard from my Father I have made known to you. You did not choose me, but I chose you and appointed you that you should go and bear fruit and that your fruit should abide, so that whatever you ask the Father in my name, he may give it to you. These things I command you, so that you will love one another' (John 15:12-17).

To be sure, we are Jesus' friends. However, to say that we experience friendship with Jesus is more than a little misleading. When comparing our relationship with Him to what we share with others, we find important similarities and dissimilarities. Therefore, to apply the concept of a mutual relationship of love, trust, and loyalty flatly to Jesus misrepresents the nature of our connection with Him that borders on blasphemy. D. A. Carson asserts, 'mutual, reciprocal friendship of the modern variety is not in view, and cannot be without demeaning God.'[8] In other words, Jesus is a friend to us in ways that we cannot be a friend to Him.

The asymmetry surfaces in this text when Jesus refers to their responsibility to obey Him as a function of their relationship. The type of mutuality imbedded in a friendship with another person does not and cannot include this

---

8. D. A. Carson, *The Gospel According to John,* The Pillar New Testament Commentary. Edited by D. A. Carson, (Grand Rapids, MI: Eerdmans, 1991), p. 522.

expectation. Notice in the language that Jesus is no longer treating His disciples as servants but has stooped near to them in treating them as friends. He condescended to die for them, to reveal the Father's will to them, and to choose them. These are incredible acts of love at great cost to Him that result in benefit for them (and us). Yet nowhere, either in this passage or in any other biblical text, does God (either the Father or the Son) invite us to treat Him as a friend. Once again, the directive for the disciples in this passage is to obey Jesus and obedience is not a healthy characteristic of mutual friendship.

The second pertinent passage in John's Gospel comes near the end in 21:15-19. In this well-known text, Jesus restores Peter following his denials and then commissions him as a leading under-shepherd for His flock of followers. While pregnant with meaning and significance for pastors, the general flow of this story demonstrates the one-sidedness of their relationship. Jesus comes to Peter, treats him as a friend in forgiving and restoring him, and then re-commissions him. Peter, as a recipient of Jesus' befriending grace, is right to respond in surrender and obedience. Jesus is a friend to Peter. Peter is a servant of Jesus.

If this is true, what do we make of Jesus being called the 'friend of tax collectors and sinners'? For starters, the quote comes from the religious leaders and is intended to be pejorative. But even still, the friendship is one-sided. Jesus is befriending them in ways that they were not invited to return. Some may also wonder about the fact that the Bible speaks of God's relationship to Abraham in similar terms. The word friendship is never used in the narrative in Genesis, but three later passages refer to him as a 'friend of God.'[9] Consistent with the language of John 15, the relationship between them is clearly asymmetrical. God is condescending to treat Abraham as a friend in choosing, saving, and blessing him while Abraham cannot, should not, and does not reply in kind.

How does this example help us understand the necessity of friendship? Jesus' demonstration of friendship to Peter (and the disciples) coupled with His command for him (and them) to love the way He loved them implies a command for friendship. Once again, we find aspects of friendship in the way He treats His disciples that we do not reciprocate. His side of the relationship is all grace leading to condescension, sacrificial love, and substitutionary death. Our side is surrender and obedience. He is a friend to us, but He is also Lord to us. Therefore, He is not offering mutual friendship, but in His relating to us provides a model for friendship in how we relate to one another. His relationship to Peter, then, is more than friendship while displaying a perfect model of it. Moreover, the corresponding command of John 15:12 to 'love one another as I have loved you,' implies that we follow this example in treating one another as friends as well. More on that command later, but for now, suffice it to say, we follow His example of love, while not every expression of it, in building relationships with others. Therefore, the command for friendship springs from, but does not perfectly mirror His friendship to us.

---

9. 2 Chronicles 20:7, Isaiah 41:8, and James 2:23.

## The Explicit Command in Directives about Human Relationships

Once again, you'll search in vain for a Bible text that explicitly commands friendship by name, but the concept is unequivocally commended. The most direct language approaching exhortation can be found in the description of proper human relationships in Old Testament wisdom literature and in the admonitions for believers in the New Testament epistles. Let's take them in turn.

'Hebrew wisdom is a category of literature that is unfamiliar to most modern Christians.'[10] The content and style significantly distance it from our context, yet the message is as relevant today as ever for understanding God's world and how we are to live in it. Most basically, the Hebrew word translated 'wisdom' refers to skill, expertise, or masterful understanding.[11] While it can be regarded objectively as God's established and observable order in the physical and social world, it's most often used in a subjective sense as the ability to live God's way in God's world which is acquired as a divine gift.[12] To this end, the word refers to skill in a variety of contexts in the Bible including: artistry,[13] government,[14] administration of justice, and even

---

10. Gordon D. Fee and Douglas Stuart, *How to Read the Bible for All Its Worth.* (Grand Rapids, MI: Zondervan, 2003), p. 225.

11. Bruce Waltke, *The Book of Proverbs: Chapters 1-15, The New International Commentary on the Old Testament.* Edited by R.K. Harrison and Robert L. Hubbard. (Grand Rapids, MI: Eerdmans, 2004), p. 76.

12. John Kitchen, *Proverbs,* A Mentor Commentary. (Ross-Shire: Christian Focus, 2006), p. 38.

13. Exodus 28 and 31.

14. Jeremiah 50:35.

diplomacy.[15] However, when examining its use in the Bible's wisdom literature, it conveys primarily a sense of religious, ethical, social, and spiritual ability that is captured well in the word virtue. Wisdom, as we use it here, is the aptitude for grasping a situation and applying God's truth so one can live in a God-honoring way.

As should be obvious, wisdom is crucial for all areas of life and especially for human relationships. Despite the complexity of nuclear physics, chemical engineering, or biomedicine, interpersonal skills present seemingly the most vexing challenges. Thus, in the three Old Testament books devoted to wisdom, human relationships occupy significant space. Job, Proverbs, and Ecclesiastes 'share wisdom as a common theme, but they wrestle with it in fundamentally different ways.' John Kitchen continues, 'Where Proverbs uses periods, Job and Ecclesiastes use question marks. Proverbs sees life as calculable, predictable, almost mathematical, while Job sees it as undecipherable and Ecclesiastes as pointless.'[16] These companions are best understood together as giving a full-orbed view of how best to live in God's world.

The pictures they paint are refreshing and discouraging in their realism, nuance, and variety. Ecclesiastes, which offers so little optimism on the whole, celebrates the value of friendship in one of its more well-known passages.

'Two are better than one, because they have a good reward for their toil. For if they fall, one will lift up his fellow. But woe to him who is alone when he falls and has

---

15. 1 Kings 5:7.

16. Kitchen, *Proverbs*, p. 18.

not another to lift him up! Again, if two lie together, they keep warm, but how can one keep warm alone? And though a man might prevail against one who is alone, two will withstand him—a threefold cord is not quickly broken.'[17]

Amidst the vanity in the world, the preacher acknowledges the practical benefit of mutual support and strength against the vulnerability of aloneness. We need others to lean on and help us in trying times. Job's reference to friendship begins promisingly as Eliphaz, Bildad, and Zophar arrive to comfort him in suffering. All goes well, that is, until they open their mouths. They act as friends but they're devoid of the wisdom necessary to provide the help Job needs. It's an example, though, of the beautiful realism in the biblical wisdom writings. These authors neither conceal nor glamorize the type of disappointments that inevitably attend to friendship.

The largest contribution of wisdom for friendship comes in Proverbs. The pithy parts of Proverbs pack a punch because they compress truth into one-liners and vivid images that prefer the power of succinctness over the clarity of long windedness.[18] Among the many lessons in this book, those related to friendship are prominent throughout. The most common Hebrew word for 'friend' used more than thirty times, but not always translated as such, can refer in a more general way to a fellow or neighbor. Rather than command the son to 'make friends,' the writers assume human relationships and give emphasis to helping him develop meaningful ones while navigating the ups and

---

17. Ecclesiastes 4:9-12.

18. Kitchen, *Proverbs*, p. 29.

downs they inevitably bring. As we'll see in the next two chapters, the specific passages related to friendship describe it more than they prescribe it. The overall picture of human relationship provided in Proverbs commends friendship as necessary for wise living without overtly commanding it. In other words, based on the vision for it in Proverbs, a person would be hard-pressed to live in a spiritually, morally, or socially skillful way without the blessing of friends.

Similarly, the New Testament directs believers toward intimate relationships of love, trust, and loyalty in the context of the local church, even if omitting the term 'friend.' While our salvation from sin is deeply personal, it's never presented as private. Each one of us must trust fully in Christ to receive forgiveness from sin, escape from God's wrath, and find reconciliation with Him. But no one is saved in isolation. The corporate or, better, the family nature of the local church permeates the biblical writings. Take, for example, Paul's letter to the Church at Ephesus. After proclaiming our salvation as a doxology and recounting our delivery from sin by grace through faith, he explains the union of Jews and Gentiles in Christ. Not only are we joined to others in Him, we are united even to those who are the most unlike us in physical characteristics and cultural background. He proceeds, in the more practical second half of the letter, to apply this overarching truth in terms of a general unity of the Spirit that binds the members of every local church together. In our salvation we become part of God's family by adoption. Building from this new position, we are called to unite with a specific family (or local church) in interconnectedness characterized by love, trust, and loyalty.

We could speak broadly about these relationships as 'community,' but they must be individual and personal at the same time. The church is not merely a group of people who assemble for congregational activities; it's a collection of people who are spiritually woven to one another. Even more than the descriptions of our being bound together, the New Testament is replete with commands for how individual believers are to relate specifically to other individual believers. One way of examining these relationships is through the 'one anothers,' or the passages that use this terminology to expressly commend mutual action between Christians. Note from this sample how our definition of friendship is reflected in these commands.

Our relationships in the church family should express intimacy.

Therefore welcome one another as Christ has welcomed you, for the glory of God (Rom. 15:7).

Greet one another with a holy kiss (Rom. 16:16). (See also 1 Cor. 16:20 and 1 Thess. 5:26).

Show hospitality to one another without grumbling. As each has received a gift, use it to serve one another, as good stewards of God's varied grace (1 Pet. 4:9-10).

Therefore, confess your sins to one another and pray for one another, that you may be healed (James 5:16).

These intimate relationships should be grounded in love.

A new commandment I give to you, that you love one another: just as I have loved you, you also are to love one another (John 13:34). (See also John 15:12, 17; Rom. 12:10; 1 Thess. 4:9; 1 Peter 1:22; 1 John 3:11, 23; 4:7, 11, 12; 2 John 5).

Therefore let us not pass judgment on one another any longer, but rather decide never to put a stumbling block or hindrance in the way of a brother (Rom. 14:13).

Only do not use your freedom as an opportunity for the flesh, but through love serve one another (Gal. 5:13).

Let us not become conceited, provoking one another, envying one another (Gal. 5:26).

Be kind to one another, tenderhearted, forgiving one another, as God in Christ forgave you (Eph. 4:32).

But if you bite and devour one another, watch out that you are not consumed by one another (Gal. 5:15).

And let us consider how to stir up one another to love and good works (Heb. 10:24).

These intimate relationships should operate by mutual trust.

Bear one another's burdens, and so fulfill the law of Christ. (Gal. 6:2).

Therefore, having put away falsehood, let each one of you speak the truth with his neighbor, for we are members one of another (Eph. 4:25).

Do not lie to one another (Col. 3:9).

Put on then, as God's chosen ones, holy and beloved, compassionate hearts, kindness, humility, meekness, and patience, bearing with one another and, if one has a complaint against another, forgiving each other; as the Lord has forgiven you, so you also must forgive. (Col. 3:12-13).

Therefore encourage one another with these words (1 Thess. 4:18).

Therefore encourage one another and build one another up, just as you are doing (1 Thess. 5:11).

These intimate relationships should continue in loyalty.

Outdo one another in showing honor (Rom. 12:10).

Live in harmony with one another (Rom. 12:16) (see also Romans 15:5).

But God has so composed the body, giving greater honor to the part that lacked it, that there may be no division in the body, but that the members may have the same care for one another (1 Cor. 12:24-25).

Let the word of Christ dwell in you richly, teaching and admonishing one another in all wisdom, singing psalms and hymns and spiritual songs, with thankfulness in your hearts to God (Col. 3:16).

And do not get drunk with wine, for that is debauchery, but be filled with the Spirit, addressing one another in psalms and hymns and spiritual songs, singing and making melody to the Lord with your heart, giving thanks always and for everything to God the Father in the name of our Lord Jesus Christ, submitting to one another out of reverence for Christ (Eph. 5:18-21).

But exhort one another every day, as long as it is called 'today', that none of you may be hardened by the deceitfulness of sin (Heb. 3:13).

Clothe yourselves, all of you, with humility toward one another, for 'God opposes the proud but gives grace to the humble' (1 Pet. 5:5).

Do not speak evil against one another, brothers (James 4:11).

Do not grumble against one another (James 5:9).

The list is not exhaustive and does not include similarly angled exhortations that omit the 'one another' phrasing. These are the tip of the larger iceberg. In addition, many of these overlap with two or more of the four categories we use to define friendship. Thus, our purpose stands because these verses demonstrate unmistakably that God commands every believer to live in ways that will yield intimate relationships of love, trust, and loyalty. By cumulative effect, then, the New Testament epistles command us to make friends.

## Conclusion

On the one hand, it borders on patronizing to present these straightforward deductions and rudimentary conclusions: God made us for friendship, Jesus modeled friendship, and God commands friendship. We simply cannot take the Bible seriously and avoid friendship. However, we know too many pastors who labor in isolation to the detriment of their souls, their families, and their ministries. These men operate as if they are either unaware of, or exempt from, this command for a host of insufficient reasons. Before confronting these challenges to friendship, we celebrate the blessings it brings.

# 5

# THE BLESSINGS OF FRIENDSHIP

Philosopher, economist, and social theorist, Jeremy Bentham, is generally credited with developing the motivational metaphor of the stick and carrot. The stick uses negative motivation through the promise of consequence for poor performance while the carrot uses positive motivation to attach reward to good performance. We don't buy it as a comprehensive system for explaining or guiding behavior, but on a simple level it presents truth of the natural world. While our internal motivations are complex and affected by the spiritual problems of our depravity, on some levels we are driven by these types of external stimuli. The threat of punishment and promise of reward are means God uses to restrain evil in general and to guide people. This is evident in the letters to the seven churches in the early chapters of Revelation, which contain a number of warnings and incentives. In this vein, we employ both to foster friendship. The next chapter is a stick aimed at prodding in the direction of submission to God's design in obedience to His implicit and explicit commands. But first, we hold out the carrot by dangling the blessings of friendship.

## Wisdom and Perspective

The Tesla brand electric vehicle uses advanced technology in creative ways to increase energy efficiency and enhance the traveling experience. From lithium-ion commodity cell batteries to driver-assistance systems and self-driving capabilities, these cars have a unique combination of previous developments and innovations. The self-driving system, for example, integrates exterior cameras, ultrasonic sensors, and a specially designed computer chip to produce self-driving capability.[1] And even when the human driver is in full control of the vehicle, this system virtually eliminates the commonly known blind spot because the car sees what the driver cannot. The concept of covering another's blind spot is not a twenty-first century technological improvement limited to automobiles; God designed friendship to do the same.

Walking alone is downright dangerous. Consider a simple syllogism: If no one is wise enough on his own and counsel is a source of wisdom, then living without counsel exposes a person to danger. Proverbs makes this case forcefully and consistently. Most commentators divide the book into seven collections based on shifts in style, changes in the material's source, or transitional cues, but the most

---

1. Michael Barnard, *If GM/Cruise Is Way Behind Waymo, How Does It Compare To Tesla?*, (20 June 2019). https://cleantechnica.com/2019/06/20/if-gm-cruise-is-way-behind-waymo-how-does-it-compare-to-tesla/. Accessed 29 June 2021.

significant move comes between chapters nine and ten. While the average Bible reader generally thinks this book contains only a collection of 'short, artistically constructed ethical observations,' the book's first section (chapters 1–9) is composed of poems in praise of wisdom that call the son to value, receive, and apply wisdom.[2] These long discourses form a single unit to instruct and nurture believers in wisdom, laying groundwork for the shorter forms that follow. In fact, without the context of this opening section, the meaning and significance of the short statements cannot be properly understood.[3] These opening poems celebrate and affirm the necessity of wisdom.

Without doubt, 'the family was the first locus of wisdom in Israelite culture' as the home rather than the school is 'presented as the primary place of training.'[4] To this end, Proverbs is most directly a commendation of wisdom from parents to their children as evident not only in the nearly two dozen uses of 'my son' but in the way the book opens. After defining wisdom in verses 2 through 7 using synonymous expressions and a reference to a proper relationship to God, Solomon addresses his son straightforwardly beginning in verse 8. While these first chapters cover a range of specific areas of life—from associations with bad company to the temptation to sexual sin—the unifying theme is the value and necessity of wisdom. And though the home is the proper launching point for the journey to gain it, the pursuit

---

2. Duane Garrett, *Proverbs, Ecclesiastes, Song of Songs,* The New American Commentary, Vol. 14. Edited by E. Ray Clendenen (Nashville, TN: Broadman & Holman, 1993), p. 29.

3. Kitchen, *Proverbs,* p. 30.

4. Garrett, *Proverbs, Ecclesiastes, Song of Songs,* p. 23-4.

cannot stop at the threshold. No one can flourish in God's world without wisdom, and as Proverbs demonstrates, other people, including parents and peers, are a source of it.

Lateral wisdom—or that which comes from a peer—shapes a person powerfully. Even subconsciously, we adopt the words, actions, and habits of the people who live most closely to us. It's well-documented that 'bad company ruins good morals,'[5] but the reverse effect occurs when both parties pursue wisdom concurrently. For example, in noting that 'whoever walks with the wise becomes wise,' the reader is challenged to select companions well for the sake of walking in wisdom.[6] This 'constant exposure to those who are wise will have a residual effect upon one's life.'[7]

The gain from wise friends is more overt when they counsel us along the way. In fact, as Garrett paraphrases Proverbs 27:9, 'parties are fun for a while, but everyone needs an earnest friend.'[8] Kitchen adds further nuance in commenting on the same verse by summarizing its commendation to 'indulge yourself in deeper levels of friendship with those God has sovereignly placed about you' in the same way we 'indulge in simple luxuries of life.'[9] In other words, the outward agreeableness of an acquaintance cannot compare with the lasting sweetness of a true friend, who, through his advice, is a consistent instrument of God's grace.

---

5. 1 Corinthians 15:33. Scholars believe Paul is quoting from the Greek poet, Menander.

6. Proverbs 13:20.

7. Kitchen, *Proverbs*, p. 294.

8. Garrett, *Proverbs, Ecclesiastes, Song of Songs*, p. 217.

9. Kitchen, *Proverbs*, p. 609.

The presence of a godly friend and even his vocalization of counsel will not make us wise any more than an unused gym membership and personal training program will make us fit. We must 'listen to advice and accept instruction' to 'gain wisdom in the future.'[10] This word reminds us that 'wisdom comes through the willingness to humbly extend our arms and embrace as a gift' the counsel and correction of another. Many pastors fail to hear, heed, internalize, and apply warnings and direction that could spare heartache and contribute to their ministry because they fail to cultivate friendship.

The gravity of the need increases for pastors, who are charged with shepherding God's people. By God's design, 'plans are established' and succeed rather than fail through the means of counsel.[11] What pastor would deny his need for practical, intellectual, and moral guidance to shape his character, inform his decisions, steer his life, and strengthen his leadership? In word, we imagine no pastor would refute it, but in practice many ignore a critical source of it; namely, friendship. More than perhaps anyone else, our task exceeds our ability. While we readily admit that, we often live in contradiction to it. Prayerful dependence on the Spirit and the resources of Scripture provide the most essential tools for our work. We have no power in which to minister and nothing worthy to say without them. Even though these supplies are sufficient for us, wisdom and perspective are God-ordained conduits for making full use of them. They have no lack, but we cannot

---

10. Proverbs 19:20.

11. Proverbs 15:22 and 20:18.

and will not reap the benefit of them fully without the help of godly friends.

The pastor who spurns God's gift of friendship displays an alarming overconfidence in his ability to serve and lead that will prevent his congregation from flourishing.

Finally, we pastors can assume the friendships we need to provide wisdom will only come in the form of other pastors. After all, they can relate to our calling and the specific challenges of it, and their past experiences more directly relate to our present situation. This logic is certainly true and pastor-to-pastor friendship is vital. Through denominational partnerships, church networks, proximity of ministry field, seminary connections, and conference engagements, invest time and energy looking for and developing friendships with other pastors who can offer wisdom. Do not neglect this vital avenue for wisdom. Be careful not to limit your friendships, however, to other men in ministry. While the laymen in your congregation cannot speak to every area of your life and ministry—like confidential counseling situations—they offer a unique and critical perspective for family life and ministry. Wisdom is not confined to seminary classrooms or formal training outlets so expect this grace to come from friends without ministry backgrounds.

## The Blessing of Support

A quintessential, biblical picture of supportive friends appears in Exodus 17 in the story of the Israelite defeat of Amalek. As we noted in chapter one, Aaron and Hur undergird Moses' leadership figuratively and literally as they hold up his arms during the battle. Biblical and church history prove that no man will persevere well in pastoral ministry without the grace of friends to walk beside him.

Our need for support is magnified by adversity as our lowest moments highlight the necessity of leaning on others. Proverbs identifies the two most likely sources of support in these difficult times: family and friends. Proverbs 17:17 presents them synonymously, 'A friend loves at all times, and a brother is born for adversity.' Some commentators read the parallelism as antithetical or contrasting, but comparison makes more sense. A friend, like a relative, persists during even our most difficult days. In fact, as Waltke notes, 'the true nature of love expresses itself by substantive, unselfish action in adversity, not by outward kisses.'[12] To this end, we know our relatives by virtue of our birth, but a crisis reveals the genuine friend.[13]

In contrast to the comparative uselessness of acquaintances, the true friend mirrors a brother in terms of commitment during difficulty.[14] Fewer friends with deeper ties will anchor life more securely than an abundance of loosely tethered associations. We must resist the temptation to dismiss the place of friendships because of our experience with casual relationships built on social conveniences that do not persevere in trials.[15] Rather, persist in pursuing friendships to enjoy the blessing of support the true ones bring.

---

12. Waltke, *The Book of Proverbs*, p. 57.

13. Kitchen, *Proverbs*, p. 382.

14. Proverbs 18:24.

15. Kitchen, *Proverbs*, p.408

The commendation to befriend another in Proverbs 27:10 affirms the value of support in calamity. This verse 'envisions a situation where [a person] suffers sudden, calamitous damage, loss, and destruction and commands him to claim the help of a tried and tested friend of the family.'[16] Kitchen rightly applies this proverb as 'an encouragement to cultivate friendships ... so that in the days of need you may find the immediate support you need.'[17] In awareness of Jesus' promise in John 16:33 that 'In the world you will have tribulation,' the need for friends becomes obvious. We cannot maintain ourselves in the smooth sailing on calm waters and will certainly sink amidst the tumultuous, stormy ones. Brothers, find faithful friends; you're going to need them.

Some suffering we face is common to all believers: financial stresses, emotional struggles, family concerns, health crises, and spiritual challenges. We all need God's sustaining grace through these and other weights that burden us in life. But pastors face added and peculiar ones as well. The weekly grind of ministering to others and sharing in their griefs and sorrows, the concern for their individual and corporate spiritual good, the unrealistic expectations of others, the disappointment of our failures, and the pressures of near-constant readiness combine to saddle us with a weight too heavy to bear. Pastoral ministry is not the only taxing vocation, but it ranks high on the list. For this reason, we need others to act as God's instruments to stabilize us—as

---

16. Waltke, *The Book of Proverbs*, p. 379.

17. Kitchen, *Proverbs*, p. 610.

Aaron and Hur did for Moses—when our strength falters in the battle.

## The Blessing of Sanctification

One of the most difficult tasks in premarital counseling is convincing the couple that a central objective of marriage is sanctification. In comparing the husband-wife relationship to that of Christ and the Church, Paul teaches this truth in Ephesians 5. He directs the husband to mirror the sanctifying love of Jesus in his relationship to his respective wife. This directive teaches the husband by implication that marriage is an avenue for him to grow in Christlikeness as well. Thus, marriage is a gift from God for sanctification and not self-fulfillment. The counter-cultural nature of this truth, however, prevents many couples from grasping the nature and significance of it. Couples need much less convincing when they end up back in the counseling room a few years into marriage. Of all the purposes God accomplishes in and through marriage, sanctification is often the most prominent and surprising.

The overlap of marriage and friendship (discussed in chapter one) shines through in this way as well. On the most basic level, we know that 'all things work together for good' for God's people.[18] This promise guarantees that every circumstance in life advances us toward glorification, even if we cannot see that connection. So of course, friendship, like everything else in life, is for our sanctification. But as

---

18. Romans 8:28.

in marriage, the correlation between friendship and growth in holiness is direct and obvious. Famously, Proverbs invoke the image of a blacksmith to illustrate this point. 'Iron sharpens iron, and one man sharpens another.'[19] This powerful, and often painful, work happens in the context of intimate relationships characterized by love, trust, and loyalty. The smelting of terrestrial ore by hand to form a smooth blade or edge is an appropriate image for the painful yet fruitful process of developing character and wisdom.[20]

A friend not only dabbles in constructive criticism but persists in it for the sake of another. In contrast to the 'fawning neighbor and quarrelsome wife, the friend performs an indispensable task.'[21] The proverbs add that direct and honest confrontation, even when severe, is more caring than the silence of cowardly affection. 'Open rebuke' and 'the wounds of a friend'[22] surpass the 'phony expressions' and 'hollow displays' of flattery.[23] True love builds up another through the painful process of shaping through confrontation. Just as the forging and finishing of a blade disrupts the iron's original form on the way to something better, so character refinement comes painfully and fruitfully on the anvil of friendship. 'Open, loving rebuke is potent; hidden love is impotent.'[24]

Pastors can be especially gun-shy in this area. Like everyone else, we enjoy congratulations more than

---

19. Proverbs 27:17.

20. Waltke, *The Book of Proverbs*, p. 384.

21. Waltke, *The Book of Proverbs*, p. 384.

22. *Proverbs* 27:5-6.

23. Garrett, *Proverbs, Ecclesiastes, Song of Songs*, pp. 216-7.

24. Waltke, *The Book of Proverbs*, p. 375.

confrontation, and we tend to be magnets for warranted and unwarranted criticism. Thus, our natural proclivity for avoiding rebuke multiplies to dangerous levels after the wounds from unfaithful adversaries come draped in friendly clothing. Pastors receive their fair share of nastygrams, and almost all of them come from church members. These notes of disapproval and complaint usually arrive anonymously, but their specificity pins them on someone with proximity to our ministry. This destructive criticism makes us even more apprehensive about the thought of 'open rebuke.' The weight of ministry also combines with our insecurities to foster gravitation toward flattery. We don't want the flaws we are most aware and ashamed of repeated back to us, even when we need it.

The antidote for the discouragement of criticism is not avoidance altogether. Rather, we need the right and loving combination of uplifting words and constructive admonition coming from a friend. God's Spirit working through His Word to apply truth to our hearts and lives continues as the dominant means for shaping and sharpening His people, and friendship is often the plate upon which this meal is served. 'Friendship with a fool is impossible' because a 'true friend does not shrink from correcting' and only the wise will receive it.[25] This blessing is also a two-way street. Not only does the friend help to sanctify us, but we are blessed by contributing directly to God's work in another person. For pastors, this gives a personal connection to the practical fruit of word-based ministry as we can see transformation in the lives of people

---

25. Waltke, *The Book of Proverbs*, p. 375.

we are shepherding. Their growth in response to friendship can fuel the fire of our sanctification as well.

Pastors, we must continue growing spiritually, striving, by God's power, for greater holiness through character formation and obedience. Despite the hours we invest in studying the Bible for our public preaching ministry and in applying the Word through the private ministry of pastoral care, 'Jesus, the Bible, and me' won't cut it. Kitchen summarizes powerfully, 'No man can be his best or reach the heights God intends for him without those blessed friends who comfort, provoke, challenge, rebuke, chide, affirm, stimulate, and encourage until his thinking is clear, his wisdom mature, his purpose refined, and his faculties sharp.'[26] The profuse kisses from the insincere, hypocritical, and deceitful sycophant may feel better in the moment, but they will only blunt the mindfulness of our sin and our alertness to danger. For the sake of your soul, brothers, pursue friendship.

## Particular Blessings for Pastors

Pliers will tighten a nut on a bolt, but a ratcheting socket wrench is always better. The specificity and precision provide for superior torque and free energy from devotion to grip strength allowing for more power applied to leverage. Take it from less-than-novice handymen, in this as in almost any example, the right tool makes the job much easier. Friendship is a blessing to any and every person. All of us need wisdom, support, and help in our sanctification, but nowhere do the benefits of friendship seem more

---

26. Kitchen, *Proverbs*, p. 616.

specifically suited than for pastors. It's a perfect balm for what ails us; it's the right tool for the job of sustaining a pastor.

Friendship combats the isolation that vocational ministry can cause for the pastor. The nature of the task tends to separate us from the 'ordinary' lives of our congregants. All human work connects to the Creator as a stewardship of His gifts and resources. We may call some employment secular, but that can only mean its immediate outputs—like auto parts, hotel reservations, or weather reports—are pertaining to the physical world primarily and not overtly to the spiritual realm. And while all our work must be done 'for the Lord' as all of it reflects Him,[27] pastoral ministry is more blatantly spiritual. We deal in souls, both their salvation and preservation. Even among high-pressure, life-and-death type jobs, ours is somewhat different. If the airplane pilot or the surgeon fails, people will die. If we fail, people will perish.[28] Therefore, our work places us in a different emotional realm than many people operate in from day to day.

In addition, friendship addresses the unique relational spaces that vocational ministry creates for pastors. Driven by self-preservation and pride, some will maintain distance from us. At the same time, we can contribute to this separation by projecting an image of self-righteousness that fails to demonstrate our awareness of the need for grace in

27. Colossians 3:23-24.

28. We hold to the historic Reformed doctrines of grace acknowledging God's sovereignty over all things, including individual salvation. Thus, we do not presume the place of saving people from sin. Nevertheless, we feel the weight of men's souls in our vocation in ways unmatched by others.

our personal lives. When the men in our churches think we live on a different spiritual plane, it discourages openness to friendship with us. This is a fine line, of course, because we must live exemplary lives as pastors while clarifying that any difference between ours and theirs comes from our dependence on God and His grace. Even still, this factor can leave the pastor feeling alone in a crowd of congregants.

These factors that unintentionally distance us from our congregations make it more and not less important for pastors to develop meaningful friendships. Because a pastor cannot overcome the separation from some members completely, cultivating a small number of intimate relationships of love, trust, and loyalty will protect him from 'aloneness.' The benefit is not unique to us; friendship is necessary for tethering us to the local church and combating the temptation to relate in an entirely superficial manner. Without friendship, a pastor can default to more of a service-provider relationship with everyone and miss the joy of knowing and being known by his church family.

Our friendships can stave off the consequences of our isolationism that affect our families as well. We can lead them to develop similarly surface-level relationships that will damage their spiritual lives and fracture their love for and relationship to the local church. The detrimental effects of a pastor's lack of friendship reverberate in his wife and children, often manifesting as resentment over feeling unloved by the church. In addition, a pastor's family may become embittered by watching him shrivel emotionally and spiritually for lack of supportive and sanctifying friends. The weight of worrying about him can sink the deep roots of cynicism and animosity toward the church that are difficult to uproot. A pastor's failure in friendship also saddles his wife with the role of confidante and counselor. We share the burden of ministry as a couple and even when she supports him well, the role is too great for any one person to sustain.

A band of faithful friends surrounding and supporting the pastor, therefore, has a powerful effect on his family. His wife and children, energized by these expressions of love, develop a strong gratitude for and commitment to the local church. They are more likely to thrive relationally themselves and to endure the trials of hostility from some members of the congregation when they witness men surrounding and loving their husband or father well. As in many areas, our families will follow our lead in developing the friendships they need. Brothers, for the sake of your family, pursue friendship.

Friendship can keep a pastor in the game. Longevity in ministry is no accident; it comes by the work of God through the means of grace. Pastors fail to persevere for a variety of reasons, but a few of them—discouragement from ineffectiveness, collapse from exhaustion, stumbling in immorality—are clearly connected to the benefits of friendship. The skill to navigate, the strength to endure, and the protection of shipwreck blossom on the tree of friendship. Brothers, for the sake of your ministry, pursue friendship.

## Conclusion

We began Part 2 asserting our obligation to pursue friendship as an act of obedience to Christ and an act of self-sacrificial love for another person. Our primary motivation in this, as in all things, is the glory of God. But as the example of Jesus' teaching in the Sermon on the Mount confirms, we can and should point to the rewards that follow our obedience. The opening statements (or Beatitudes) pair a kingdom expectation with a kingdom blessing to show that the practicing of righteousness (through prayer, fasting, and giving) results in reward from the Father when done according to His command. Following His lead, we exhort you, brothers, to consider the blessings that flow from friendship and allow them to spur you on.

# 6

# THE CHALLENGES OF FRIENDSHIP

Watching a person make a difficult task look easy is beautiful. We marvel when the painter's seemingly chaotic brushstrokes take shape, the golfer's ball lands exactly where he aimed, or the preacher weaves exposition, illustration, and application together seamlessly and powerfully. We may associate art with drawing, sculpting, painting, and the like, but proficiency in any applied skill is 'artistic' and worthy of admiration. Consider the incredible difficulty of connecting with a 100 mph fastball from just over sixty feet with a required response time of less than half a second to hit a home run, or of mastering a musical instrument by grasping music theory and applying the physical dexterity to produce symphonic delight. These are not easy tasks, but some people sure make it look that way. Similarly, and to my amazement, some people make friendship look easy when it isn't.

Friendship is hard in nearly every circumstance because the components are unnatural. Intimacy requires vulnerability, but we're natural hiders. Every description of love in 1 Corinthians 13 requires the Holy Spirit because we cannot muster any on our own. Trust requires overcoming innate and experientially justified skeptical intuitions. Loyalty requires a selflessness outside our default inclinations. In addition, pastoral ministry adds yet another degree of difficulty because our calling can foster isolation, pride, and distrust of others. This fact gives no ground for excuse or self-pity, but facing the reality provides a path toward healthy relationships.

In this chapter, we diagnose the problems that contribute to mankind's aversion to friendship while highlighting factors that increase the difficulty for pastors. We group them into three categories—external obstacles to engagement, internal obstacles to engagement, and obstacles to perseverance—and lean on wisdom from Proverbs to define and describe them. Some result from sinful circumstances while others emerge from sinful impulses, but all contribute to the failure of many pastors to invest in building deep, meaningful friendships.

## External Obstacles to Engagement

'Every good gift and every perfect gift is from above, coming down from the Father of lights, with whom there is no variation or shadow due to change.'[1] 'If you then, who are evil, know how to give good gifts to your children, how much more will your Father who is in heaven give good things to those who ask him!'[2] The Scriptures sufficiently articulate and substantiate God's kindness in giving to His

---

1. James 1:17.
2. Matthew 7:11.

children. Friendship, which flows from Him to us, is one of these good gifts. The most natural response, then, would be to receive it, embrace it, and enjoy it. Unfortunately, it rarely happens that smoothly for a variety of reasons.

One factor that contributes to the refusal to enjoy the gift of friendship is evident in the story of Genesis 3. The Adversary lures the first people away from God's design by a cunning strategy of creating doubt in God's goodness and in the quality and sufficiency of His provision. He uses a similar tactic when it comes to friendship: namely, he misrepresents and degrades the gift to pull us away from it and into isolation. To this end, there is a modern assault on friendship. While we can be confident that every generation faced obstacles to developing and sustaining these relationships, a set of unique challenges has emerged in the past several decades. Friendship has been misunderstood, purposefully redefined, and at times intentionally devalued. These frontal assaults on friendship include a hollowing out of the term, a depersonalizing of the concept, lack of good options, competition for relational space in our lives, and an oversexualization of all relationships.

Colloquial expressions reveal deeply-held values in the culture. The phrases 'blood is thicker than water' and 'just friends' convey sentiments that indirectly expose a diminished view of friendship that is pervasive in our context. In both cases, the primary intent centers on the elevation of one type of relationship through the means of relative value. The first expression emphasizes the loyalty of a familial bond while the second emphasizes the intimacy of a dating relationship. Unfortunately, and perhaps even unintentionally, friendship gets slighted in the process. Cultural values can rise and fall when ideas become embedded in common vernacular and then steer our thoughts and perceptions both consciously and subconsciously. While the false dichotomies between friendship and these other relationships may be incidental or accidental, the effect of them reverberates nonetheless. By and large, our culture views friendship as a third or fourth-tier relationship.

Social media is not the downfall of modern society, but it might be one of the locomotives that takes us there. These inventions prey on sinful impulses to fuel comparison, multiply distraction, glorify ungodliness, promote self-aggrandizement, and exacerbate relational dysfunction. This sample scratches the surface of the innumerable harms that come from these platforms, but this is no empty rant. It's pertinent for our discussion because the use of the term 'friend' for the connection among people on Facebook highlights the way these mediums assault biblical friendship. This use of the term depersonalizes the concept by reducing it to little more than acquaintanceship driven by curiosity. At times, this term is little more than a synonym for 'people I'd like to spy on every now and then.' This virtual voyeurism yields an obsession with the lives of others devoid of meaningful relational connection. Hence, they damage our desire for relationship and our capacity for building intimacy with the people physically present in our lives.

Excessive acquaintanceship is not only a symptom of our social media age, but it also often emerges from an apparent lack of good choices. Some men, especially pastors, legitimately look around and see no good options. They know the isolation of ministering in a context with very few other believing men with whom to develop meaningful friendships.

We live with limits. Unlike God, we aren't omni-anything; rather, we're bound by time, space, knowledge, ability, capacity, and so on. Thus, we are forced to manage our lives making decisions based on our priorities that lead us to leave even good things aside. In our experience of ministering beside and training pastors, we know that friendship often takes a backseat to almost everything else because failure in this area isn't as immediately apparent. Neglect your family, your sermon preparation, pastoral care, or a leadership meeting and someone will notice. Investing in relationships, however, seems deceptively rewarding because it avoids draining the already shallow pool of time and energy needed for other worthy pursuits. As is true in so many areas, we will never have time for friendship until and unless we make time for friendship.

Sexual sin pervades our culture. The temptations rise from our sinful hearts and surround us on every side. While not entirely new in human history, the recent proliferation and glorification of sexual promiscuity along with the growing acceptance of behaviors that were previously regarded as entirely immoral has been a stunning and swift cultural shift. In a span of less than twenty years, the federal government enacted and then struck down the Defense of Marriage Act, which explicitly defined marriage as a legal union between a man and a woman. While it was not unanimous, the legislation's bipartisan support in 1996 was evident in the voting record for both chambers of Congress and by the fact that it was sponsored by a Republican Congressman and signed into law by a Democratic President. In a rapid about-face, the Supreme Court struck the law down in 2013 and then rendered it superseded and unenforceable in 2015. The culture's barometer for acceptable sexual behavior has moved, and is moving, further and further from the biblical standard.

But there's more. Not only is the standard for acceptable sexual behavior shifting, the appetite for and commitment to infuse sexuality in every sphere of life is multiplying as well. Oversexualization is endemic. In the present, sexuality is now an essential aspect of every person's identity and even children are encouraged to 'identify' their sexual preferences at early ages. This aggressive insistence on sexuality taints relationships—both in the present and the past—by bringing suspicion and seeing what we'd call immorality everywhere. For example, one of the most God-honoring portraits of friendship in Scripture— that of Jonathan and David—is routinely interpreted by modern, liberal scholars as having a homosexual component. Of course, we reject those notions as devoid of any shred of biblical support, but we mention it because it demonstrates the effect of our culture's obsession with sex. The prevailing tide of public opinion is ready to impose homosexuality in every sphere of life, and the impact on friendship should be obvious. In an effort to avoid immorality or the perception of it, some men dodge meaningful relationships altogether while others limit intimacy. These unnecessary restrictions prevent some men from developing true biblical friendships. Thus, the external obstacle of errant worldviews becomes an internal one, which segues into our next section.

## Internal Obstacles to Engagement

The biggest dangers to our spiritual lives come from within. Yes, the Adversary is real and active 'prowl[ing] around like a roaring lion, seeking someone to devour.'[3] While the external hindrances to friendship deter our investment, the internal obstacles can eliminate the possibility of it completely. Diagnosing the heart allows for the prescription of a remedy. While these dangers are present for every believer, pastors are particularly susceptible to them.

### Pride

The proud are in trouble from square one. And despite the warning signs, none can escape its clutches. We pastors are well aware that 'when pride comes, then comes disgrace' and that 'pride goes before destruction, and a haughty spirit before a fall.'[4] Yet, we propagate the lie in our own minds that we can persevere in life and in ministry without help. Friendlessness grows like fruit from the root of pride because the person who is full of himself will not have friends. Arrogance can also manifest in the deception of self-sufficiency yielding a 'lonerism' that is both foolish and contradictory to the Christian's life.

Solomon and the other contributors to Proverbs are not only relentless in their assault on pride, but they speak to how it prevents friendship. For starters, pride is an enemy of friendship because the person is self-deceived and unwilling to stoop low enough to receive it. Our default setting trusts

---

3. 1 Peter 5:8.
4. Proverbs 11:2 and 16:18.

in our opinion because all our ways 'are pure in [our] own eyes.'[5] Therefore, we cling to this foolish thought jettisoning the wise path that 'listens to advice.'[6] These Old Testament sages invoke the image of the scoffer and the sluggard to land this lesson as well. The scoffer, or the one who despises correction and rebuke, 'will not go to the wise.'[7] And further, the sluggard will not hear from anyone else because he 'is wiser in his own eyes than seven men.'[8] The truth may be summarized like this: know-it-alls don't have friends because they don't want any and they feel no need for one. In this way, many pastors never pursue friendship because pride, which spills out as both arrogance and the self-deception of sufficiency, trips them at the gate.

*Fear of Man*

Rightly conceived, the fear of man is a subset of pride defined as replacing God with people and allowing what others think or what we imagine they think to control us.[9] Borrowing from Ed Welch's *When People are Big and God is Small*, we note three types of fear that lead us to adapt our lives.[10] First, we fear that another person will do harm to us if they know us well. Without question, suffering is an aspect of life in this world. While we try to protect ourselves through wisdom, especially from physical harm,

---

5. Proverbs 16:2.

6. Proverbs 12:15.

7. Proverbs 15:12.

8. Proverbs 26:16.

9. Ed Welch, *When People are Big and God is Small,* (Phillipsburg, NJ: P & R Publishing, 1997), p. 14.

10. Ed Welch, *When People are Big and God is Small,* pp. 23-72.

friendship leaves us vulnerable to emotional and relational hurt.[11] Whether intentionally or unintentionally, some will do harm to you which requires discernment and caution when entrusting ourselves to others. Even more, pastors often experience the deep pain in this regard by people who weaponize our transparency to damage our reputation and ministry.

A second manifestation of this fear stems from the dread of being exposed as a fraud. Connected to the pride of maintaining a false image before others, we refuse to remove the mask we wear to conceal our weaknesses. In this way, friendship requires acknowledging and accepting, in humility, our utter lack of impressiveness. While we should rest in the finished work of Christ and not our capability, friendship helps to press us to ground our lives and our hope in the gospel through vulnerability. Imperfection is part of human existence so the more we are known, the more it will be exposed. Disclosure in the context of friendship, which can function as an instrument of grace to shape our character, is a terrifying thought for most. The fear that our private lives will be broadcast by a lack of confidentiality acts as a deterrent, but it ought not to. While we must practice discernment to avoid entrusting ourselves to unreliable men, the risk cannot be avoided entirely. Once again, pastors know the danger of exposure because a weakness in the hands of an opponent can be used to destroy our ministry.

---

11. If a friend, or anyone, is abusing you and causing you physical harm, the proper and most loving response is not to ignore or endure it. Instead, seek safety and, with the help of others, confront the abuse and call the person to stop.

Finally, we fear man in suspecting that others will not like or accept us as they get to know us. Yet again, this scenario is altogether possible. Some people befriend us with ulterior motives seeking personal gain. With selfishness driving them, they will discard the relationship if it ceases to be beneficial. On the other hand, others may distance themselves from us because of personality quirks or even our own relational immaturity. Regardless of whether the underlying issue connects to them or to us, some friendships will not persist once we are truly known. This experience is all too common for men in pastoral ministry who invest in a friend only to face the sting of rejection. Whether realized or not, this fear stifles relational investment.

In the face of these realities, however, we must walk by faith in God relying on His sovereignty and promises. Rather than operating by self-preservation, we avoid protecting ourselves through secrecy and depend on God to defend and vindicate us at the proper time. The path to overcoming the fear of man in friendship is not personal perfection; rather, it's a road of humility grounded in the fear of God. Pastors, these relationships force us to demonstrate this lifestyle that we inevitably commend to our congregations.

*Laziness*
Friendship is hard work that many are unwilling to undertake. Laziness and passivity plague our culture. While 'there is nothing new under the sun,' the endemic levels of sloth apparent in our media-obsessed context seem like a new depth to this struggle. We know enough history to realize that members of older generations have

frequently criticized the failures of the ones behind them, but it is impossible to argue with the assertion that today's young adult would find life in the 1940s to be impossibly strenuous. Leaving the debate about relative laziness for historians and social scientists, the problem stretches back to the beginning of human history. Solomon addresses it consistently in his contribution to Proverbs.

To begin, the slack hand is condemned because it leads to forced labor, hunger, and poverty.[12] Using the image of the ant, he warns that the sluggard will always ultimately suffer, and often in the form of self-inflicted impoverishment.[13] 'Even his deepest inner longings remain vaporous dreams because he lacks the motivation to apply himself to see them become reality.'[14] Further, this brand of fool is described as restless, helpless, and useless because he has insatiable desires without the willingness to do what is necessary to attain them.[15]

While not applied to friendship directly in Proverbs, the principles are relevant for this discussion, nonetheless. Many people desire friendship in theory but will not devote themselves to the work of developing it in reality. They refuse to devote time and energy required by love. Recall, love is one of the key characteristics of friendship. This commitment to another person's good, even at great personal cost, is well beyond the reach of the relational sluggard who slumbers selfishly in isolation.[16] The person who refuses to

---

12. Proverbs 12:24, 19:15, and 10:4.

13. Proverbs 6:6-11.

14. Kitchen, *Proverbs*, p. 283.

15. Proverbs 13:4, 15:19, 10:26 and 18:9.

16. This definition of love was heavily influenced by Jonathan Leeman, *The Church and the Surprising Offense of God's Love.* (Wheaton, IL: Crossway, 2010), p. 85.

pay the price for friendship will eventually pay the price of not having a single friend. Pastors, even those who are not prone to laziness, face the temptation to avoid the work of cultivating friendship under the banner that we sacrifice in love in many other ways for our congregation.

*Weariness*

It'd be nice to have a relational energy gauge similar to a battery life indicator on a cell phone. After charging the device, the display reports the depletion of stored power in measurable increments allowing for proper management. Before reaching a point of complete battery drain, the warnings flash on the screen. Emotional weariness is neither easily measured nor reported, but it is no less real. Relationships, even those that on the whole make contributions to our lives, can be difficult and draining.

Every human relationship is challenging because each one inherently involves sinners. The more active forms of sin like harm and disappointment combined with the fact that people are tediously difficult to love make friendship work. David's anguish, expressed in Psalm 55, over his suffering at the hands of a 'friend' comes as no surprise. Lamentable as it may be, all of us have faced distress because of the actions of a friend. Peter's question of Jesus and His response about forgiveness demonstrates well that long-term relationships require a flood of grace flowing in both directions.[17] From experience as the 'disappointee' and 'disappointer,' this burden of reconciliation dissuades us from investing in friendship.

---

17. Matthew 18:21.

Added to the weight of relational wounds, the more common inconveniences of relational closeness yield another dimension of deterrent. Friendships that are not overtly or directly hurtful in any way still deplete emotional energy. Even for the more extroverted who are energized by others, relationships can be downright exhausting. The point of fatigue for pastors is difficult to see and even more difficult to avoid. Because of the nature of our work, a majority of our relational energy is spent with people who receive more from us than they contribute. This expending of ourselves to serve others wearies the soul and tempts us to cocoon when the demands of our calling allow for it.

*Selfishness*
The statement is terrible grammatically but memorably true, 'I love me some self.' The second greatest commandment invokes this fact as the means for expressing the requirement to love other people.[18] Despite some modern attempts to use the phrasing as a platform for promoting 'self-love,' God was acknowledging and not commending it. Plain ole, unadulterated love of self powerfully prevents relationships of love and loyalty that demand sacrifice. In one sense, the previous obstacles on this list are linked to this one: pride, fear of man, laziness, and weariness flow from an exorbitant commitment to self.

An aforementioned example of the opposite illustrates the point well. Remember again, the relationship between Jonathan and David. The covenant between them came at

---

18. Matthew 22:39 and Leviticus 19:18

great cost to Jonathan as his loyalty meant a forfeiture of any claim to kingship in Israel, conflict with his father, and even the threat of physical harm at times. Yet, Jonathan sacrifices for his friend in ways that work against natural human inclinations as our sinful nature defaults to taking and not giving.

Pastors, who invest significant time and energy to sacrificing for others in their ministry, fall prey to selfishness when it comes to personal friendships. Without recognizing it, we withdraw from, or avoid, the necessary intimacy they require out of self-interest. We try to justify it by pointing to our selfless displays in the realm of ministry, but the two spheres do not overlap. Sacrifice as part of our calling does not exempt us from sacrifice in friendship.

## Lack of Self-Awareness
This final obstacle differs from the previous ones in a significant regard. Rather than describing a sinful impulse from within that dissuades us from making the investment in friendship, this one arises from within but acts as a deterrent for others. Some people, and pastors are especially susceptible, display a remarkable lack of self-awareness that repels others from befriending us. Proverbs 17:27-28 illustrates this point more than asserting it.

> Whoever restrains his words has knowledge,
>> and he who has a cool spirit is a man of understanding.
> Even a fool who keeps silent is considered wise;
>> when he closes his lips, he is deemed intelligent.

When a fool opens his mouth, others detect his foolishness. Unfortunately, many pastors are blind to their relational awkwardness and even offensiveness that are readily apparent to everyone else. A variety of factors contribute to this problem for pastors, but part of it grows from isolating themselves from honest feedback and from a failure to receive criticism constructively. A true friend will persevere through this challenge to help us, but too often we refuse to embrace the reality of our problem and so they walk away. In our collective experience of training pastors, we have seen the lack of self-awareness stymie a pastor's life and ministry in a variety of areas, especially in the formation of friendship.

## Obstacles to Perseverance

No runner wins a race at the start block, but many lose it there. Particularly in a competition of sprinters, a poor start torpedoes the possibility of success. However, most races are lost somewhere along the way and not in the first few steps. Despite the many obstacles that prevent us from attempting to make a friend, those that prevent us from maintaining a friendship appear even more substantial. For friendship, which is more a marathon than a sprint, starting is necessary and difficult, but persevering borders on impossible. Many pastors will cross the hurdles to get started, but stumble on the road only to give up. We categorize the primary impediments along the way as personal foolishness, relational misfires, betrayal, and bad influence.

## Personal Foolishness

The most likely weapon of destruction in our friendships stares at us every morning in the mirror. As humans, foolishness lurks around nearly every corner of our inner lives. Once again, Proverbs highlights this reality as well as any of part of Scripture. Examining the three specific Hebrew words translated 'fool' in the text allows us to see this truth.

The most common word translated 'fool' in Proverbs (כְּסִיל) refers to someone who is dull and obstinate.[19] This person is not mentally slow, but spiritually unperceptive. He has the capability of ascertaining knowledge, but he despises it instead.[20] This word is invoked when referring to the foolishness on display in a person who talks incessantly to spew idiocy and appears only interested in listening to himself.[21]

The second most prevalent Hebrew word (אֱוִיל) used to describe the fool suggests stupidity and stubbornness.[22] He talks more than he listens and is stubborn, argumentative, and easily offended.[23] This quarrelsome and licentious person is morally bad and wreaks havoc wherever he goes.[24] The third Hebrew word (נָבָל), which is only used three times in Proverbs, adds very little but reinforces these same ideas. This person has no ethical or religious

---

19. F. Brown, S. Driver, and C. Briggs, *The Brown-Driver-Briggs Hebrew and English Lexicon*, (Peabody, MA, 2000), p. 493.

20. Derek Kidner, *Proverbs*, (Downers Grove, IL: interVarsity Press, 2008), p. 37.

21. Proverbs 15:2, 14

22. Kidner, *Proverbs*, p. 38.

23. Proverbs 10:8 and 12:15-16.

24. Proverbs 20:3 and 27:22.

perception[25] and is perhaps best described as boorish and close-minded both to God and to reason.[26] The fool, then, is overbearing and at times crude. As you can see, a fool makes a terrible friend.

The opening nine chapters of Proverbs present a series of sermonic appeals to the son in an attempt to persuade him to abandon the way of folly in favor of the way of wisdom. Starting with a properly ordered relationship to God, summarized as the 'fear of the Lord,' Solomon urges him (and by extension all of us) to walk the path consistent with God's ordering of the world. These entreaties address a broad range of life spheres, but nearly all of them are connected in some way to human relationships. The way of wisdom calls us to relate in particular and God-honoring ways to other people. But we are tempted, for many of the same reasons noted earlier, to equivocate or avoid these responsibilities. Yet, even when we pursue them, we often do so in dysfunctional ways.

By inattention or outright stupidity, our spiritual dullness and obstinance yields a pigheadedness that manifests in thin-skinned sensitivity and belligerently confrontational attitudes. For pastors in particular, the blessing of our biblical knowledge fuels an arrogance that is at best off-putting to others and at worst devastating to intimacy altogether. We would all like to think these things are true of everyone else and not of us, but the reality hits close to home. Many people, including pastors, do not have

25. F. Brown, S. Driver, and C. Briggs, *The Brown-Driver-Briggs Hebrew and English Lexicon,* p. 614.

26. Kidner, *Proverbs,* p. 38.

any friends because they are terrible friends themselves. In a strange irony, the instrument for carving foolishness out of our lives is the very thing it attacks; namely, intimate relationships of love, trust, and loyalty. Until and unless we make consistent progress in sanctification, we will struggle to maintain healthy friendships.

## Relational Misfires in Both Directions

With a few exceptions, marriage crises begin with minor fissures. By the time a struggling couple arrives in the pastor's or counselor's office, the initial point of conflict seems relatively benign and was years in the past. The eruptions that dissolve these relationships developed from small wounds that never healed allowing deeper infections to fester beneath the surface. The anomaly proves the rule that the compilation of minor issues devastates more often than an individual, major issue. What is obvious in marriage is also present in friendship; namely, these relationships dissolve because of numerous thoughtless actions that may do imperceptible harm in the moment but do irreparable damage over the long term.

Surveying Proverbs provides a suitable sample of these relational misfires. They include conversational failures like jumping to conclusions,[27] rash words,[28] stubborn defensiveness,[29] argumentativeness,[30] and taking a joke

---

27. Proverbs 18:13.

28. Proverbs 12:18.

29. Proverbs 18:19.

30. Proverbs 26:21.

too far.[31] Sociologists can debate the relative role of nonverbal communication, but thoughtless words tear friends apart. The warning that 'when words are many, transgression is not lacking' is especially relevant for friendship.[32] More generic displays of insensitivity—overstaying your welcome,[33] failure to respect a somber moment,[34] or excessive noise early in the morning[35]—also cause conflict and relational strife. While not all of these verses directly address friendship, all present relational breakdowns that are pertinent in this realm. This category of struggle is vital to address because more failed friendships are casualties of carelessness than are results of aggression.

Pastors are prone to thoughtlessness, too. We, who give attention to the precision of our words in the pulpit, can be guilty of speaking inconsiderately in casual settings. Even worse, we have observed strange and startling levels of entitlement among pastors. It strikes us as odd because we are servants of Christ and His Church, yet some men act as though church members owe them generosity because of their role. This mentality destroys trust eroding any semblance of friendship. When it comes to making and keeping friends, unfortunately some pastors are their own worst enemy owing from these types of failures.

---

31. Proverbs 26:18-19.

32. Proverbs 10:19.

33. Proverbs 25:17.

34. Proverbs 25:20.

35. Proverbs 27:14.

## Betrayal

David was surely right that bearing the taunt of an enemy is far easier than the weight of a friend's betrayal.[36] Of the four challenges we highlight here, this one likely is the most difficult to endure and the least in need of explanation. Tragically, some friendships fall by the wayside because one member of the pair acts unfaithfully toward the other, betraying the person and completely contradicting the definition of friendship.

The sting of disloyalty cuts deeply. Unearthed gossip or slander evaporates trust immediately so that few friendships can endure such foolish behavior.[37] The slanderer is a fool, but the deceit beneath the act causes an especially deep wound for the victim.[38] Passivity and silence in a moment when support is needed may appear less harmful, but the absence of aggression barely blunts the pain. Another common temptation of close relationships is for one person to maintain it for some selfish gain, only to discard it once the usefulness expires. Finally and most blatantly, outright treachery pierces the soul and extinguishes friendship.

While a pastor can find himself on both sides of betrayal, we seem to suffer as the victim more often than not. Part of it stems from the exposure of our position and we'd hope another part is our commitment to holiness. Nevertheless, the challenge with betrayal is not confined to the friend involved in that situation as

---

36. Psalm 55:12-13.

37. Proverbs 17:9.

38. Proverbs 10:18.

much as the effect it can have on other relationships. We are commanded to pursue reconciliation by extending forgiveness with otherworldly generosity, which is always difficult.[39] The greater obstacle, however, is often overcoming the temptation to allow one failure to influence every other relationship. The resulting suspicion can lead us to withdraw, harming the intimacy we had previously enjoyed with other friends.

## Bad Influence

This final challenge prevents friendships from persevering, and rightfully so. It may seem odd for a book arguing for the necessity of friendship to recommend separating from some friends, but this path follows the wisdom of Proverbs. While we addressed the blessings of friendship in the previous chapter, we noted that a believer invests with hope that it will offer mutual benefit in terms of spiritual growth. However, there will be occasions where the friend refuses to pursue Christ with zeal or seriousness. We know well that not every man who claims to know Christ by faith actually walks in obedience to Him. As noted by Solomon, some friendships will have a detrimental effect on us through their bad influence. We should, for example, avoid befriending an angry man because he will rub off on us and entangle us in his ways.[40] In the midst of working to cultivate friendships, some weeds will grow in that garden and require removal.

---

39. Matthew 18:21.

40. Proverbs 22:24-25.

## Conclusion

Friendships are difficult to sustain because they have many enemies. From the Adversary to our culture to ourselves, the path is littered with land mines stacking the odds against us. Yet, we mustn't give up because, as God's children, friendship is both a command for us and one of His good gifts to us. His commands are always for our ultimate good and His gifts are to be received by faith. But to do so will require an awareness of the challenges and a readiness by His Spirit to overcome them. Pastors, in this, as in all areas of our spiritual life, we must lead our congregations.

# 7

# MODERN EXHORTATIONS TO PASTORAL FRIENDSHIP

Indeed, J.C. Ryle was correct in noting, 'Friendship halves our troubles and doubles our joy.'[1] Despite increasing connectedness, many in our culture face a growing isolation of the soul and pastors are prime candidates for this paradoxical lifestyle. But we can't care well for the souls in our congregation if we're weary and wandering ourselves. Even though we interact with dozens of people in our churches and social media circles, we often foster few, if any, spiritual friendships. We hope by now you're convinced that this instrument of grace is vital for personal growth and pastoral longevity and are ready to commit to developing God-glorifying, Christ-exalting, Spirit-empowered friendships for the sake of your soul and those under your care.

The aim of this final chapter is to encourage each pastor to consider how he might pursue his own pastoral friendships in the days ahead. We will seek to accomplish

---

1. J. C. Ryle, *Practical Religion,* (Carlisle, PA: Banner of Truth, 2013), p. 317.

this in two ways. First, we will suggest ten exhortations on how pastors might begin to develop meaningful, trusted, and loyal friendships in their own lives. Second, we will share real, personal examples from our own lives on how ministry friendships have been a tremendous blessing, a means for spiritual growth, and have proven to be that forgotten piece to help any pastor persevere in his ministry.

## 1. Die to self

All three synoptic Gospels record the following famous words from Jesus, 'If anyone would come after me, let him deny himself and take up his cross and follow me.'[2] Selfishness impedes progress in friendship as in all other areas of spiritual growth. While we don't die for others in the way Jesus did, each of us must be prepared to 'lay down his life for his friends.'[3]

Brian: My good friend, Jim, shares a birthday with my youngest daughter. On her fifth birthday this busy pastor who lives across town showed up at my house on his birthday to bring her six specialty cupcakes from Gigi's cupcakes. My daughter got to determine which cupcake she wanted and who of our family of six got one of the other Cupcakes. As you can imagine, my friend made a lifelong friend with my daughter that day, known for many years to come as, 'Her birthday buddy!' My friend repeated this very selfless act for several years to come. This busy pastor, with his own birthday to celebrate and his own flock to care

---

2. Matthew 16:24; Mark 8:34; Luke 9:23.

3. John 15:13.

for, showed up at my front door out of love for me and my daughter for the next five plus years.

Many times, dying to self in pastoral friendship is not about some loud, dramatic sacrifice, but best illustrated by a small, thoughtful, unexpected, and intentional act of kindness. Every pastor knows one of the best ways to love a pastor is to love his family. In loving my daughter in this unique way, I felt his love for me. On my daughter's thirteenth birthday the tide turned. She showed up at Jim's church on a Wednesday night with a box full of Gigi's cupcakes, a sweet gesture of how much Jim's birthday visits had meant to her—and to me.

## 2. Invest wisely in relationships

Passivity rarely produces anything of value, but equal investments also rarely yield identical returns. Prepare for the work of befriending and pray for discernment concerning where to apply it. Not every potential friend will reciprocate and often the truest ones will come in surprising places.

Michael: Friendships take time and energy. Over the years, I have carved out time to invest in friendships, most of which have developed from a teacher-student relationship. What this has meant is purposefully contacting these friends and spending time in person with them or speaking to them over the phone or now by Zoom. I am deeply invested as an academic and it would have been easy for me to have spent this time in academic pursuits. But I knew that I needed friendships for the good of my soul. I had seen the dangers of ignoring such a need in the life of my own father, who, too, was a lifelong academic. In his case his field of study was electrical engineering. He was so focused on his vocation that he had no real time for friends. I was determined not to be like that.

## 3. Value the power of presence

Most people assume friendship is about a relationship with someone that is based on interactions, conversations, advice, wrestling through struggles, and talking through solutions. This is certainly assumed in pastoral friendships as we seek relationships with other pastors to help us wade through the tricky waters of pastoral ministry. But sometimes what we need is a friend who is willing to simply sit with us in silence, be present, and listen. There is a value in the power of presence when a human being sits with another human being to be a warm, accepting, and loving presence who listens.

Brian: One of the most important friendships in my life is with a fellow pastor—we meet for a coffee every Wednesday morning. The sole focus of this time together is to care for one another's soul. We rarely talk about ministry problems. We don't hash out solutions to church challenges. We don't discuss our sermon series we are preaching. We talk about each other. We check in on our emotional state, mental capacity, and spiritual engagement. Nothing is off limits. We can bring whatever we need to bring to each other and there is no judgment. We come together to assess the activity of our own souls before God. We best accomplish this through a single commitment to one another—presence. We are committed to come together and simply sit with one another. Sometimes one of us shares more than the other. But our commitment is to sit and listen and be present to the need of the other.

Sometimes our most meaningful friendships are not those relationships where we come together to dialogue, but those relationships that invite sitting together in silence and simply enjoying the presence of the other. That's what this friend is to me. And it is special. With the number of voices in a pastor's life, I assume all pastors would be better equipped to persevere in ministry if they had friendships that had less words and more warm presence as its foundation.

## 4. Seek friendships inside and outside the church and lead your wife to do the same

While the value of friends in the same ministry trench cannot be overstated, the addition of friends outside our particular ministry field is also important. Time and distance make these relationships more difficult to develop and maintain, but they sustain a pastor and his wife in unique and critical ways.

Brian: Some of my most meaningful pastoral friendships to this day were found outside my church context, but one of the most crucial friendships came outside my church with someone who wasn't even a pastor. As I continued to pastor a local church and lead a growing ministry to other pastors,[4] I found myself always surrounded with those who wanted me to be their pastor. I had church members looking

---

4. Practical Shepherding is my ministry to other pastors which I continue to lead as my primary ministry focus. For more information, go to www.practicalshepherding.com

to me as their pastor. And I had other pastors looking to me as a kind of pastor to them. I reached a point of exhaustion when I realized I needed a meaningful relationship with someone who didn't want me to pastor them.

My wife had felt the same need and had developed a meaningful friendship with another woman in our city, not a pastor's wife, who went to church across town. Her husband was a Chick-fil-A owner/operator and was a faithful church member. Having been at some group gatherings with him as a result of our wives' friendship, I reached out to see if he might want to spend some time together.

Over time, we developed a very meaningful friendship. He didn't want to talk about ministry. He didn't want to talk much about church stuff or theology. He wanted to eat hot wings, watch some football, talk a little politics, and share about our families. We talked about hobbies, other interests, and our own walks with the Lord as men. God used this friendship to show me two things about myself. First, how refreshing this friendship was to all my other relationships. Second, how much I needed a friendship like this to provide an environment of rest from all the other ministry and relationships tied to it that had consumed my life. His friendship is still one of the most important in my life.

## 5. Calibrate expectations

Unstated and unrealistic ones can destroy a relationship, but we needn't eliminate expectations altogether. Instead, determine the relational sphere in which a friend operates and calibrate them accordingly.

James: Like everyone else, I have many different types of friends. Some operate mostly in one sphere of life while others share in the wider experience of overlap with family, church, and recreation. With some, the intimacy and vulnerability run deep but with others, things remain much closer to the surface. These distinctions don't determine the quality of the friend, but they must affect the way we evaluate it. Nearly all will know the emotional struggle that accompanies the sting of disappointment when a friend is absent or unresponsive in time of need.

We mustn't seek to escape the pain of unmet expectations by avoiding them in isolation; rather, we must learn to set them appropriately. Some people adjust them intuitively as they move in and out of relationships, but for those who struggle with feeling let-down more regularly, this area is likely a key to healthier friendships. In these circumstances, we give too little thought to relational terms but apply them unilaterally to every friend. However, learning to establish them for each person by giving careful consideration to the level of overlap and the person's margin based on stage of life and other commitments, and the amount of investment we are making in the relationship will provide a path toward longer-term friendships.

## 6. Seek deep connection to foster trust in one another

Unintentional, relational misfires sabotages friendships. Most often, insensitivity contributes to these problems because one or both people fail to appreciate the other person's point of view. Well before the potential for conflict arises, connect with one another to grow in understanding and compassion with each other to subvert problems before and after they occur. That deep connection cultivates a trust that enables us to say hard things to someone else.

Michael: When I was in my twenties, my closest friend, apart from my wife, was a young man named Peter. We had a midweek Bible Study that met on Tuesday evenings and over a number of years we saw great fruitfulness from it. Both of us had strong links at the time to the charismatic movement. One week, Peter told me that the following Tuesday he would be teaching on the gift of speaking in tongues and that it was the doorway to the reception of all of the other gifts. Although I did not believe this, I agreed to Peter teaching this as I was afraid to disrupt our friendship. But, after he had taught this, I felt led to tell him I disagreed with him. His response was quick and acerbic. He disagreed with me in no uncertain terms. I unwisely told him that he was acting like the leader of a cult. At that, he told me that he was done with the Bible Study and I could lead it henceforth alone. He not only ceased to be involved in the Bible Study but he also stopped attending church and categorically brought our friendship to an abrupt end. I have never been able to fully understand his reaction, but I was determined not to allow this failure of one friendship to sour me on others. I knew that friendship was essential for the good of my soul.

## 7. Be gracious in offense

'Good sense makes one slow to anger, and it is his glory to overlook an offense.'[5] Good friends are quick to give the benefit of the doubt, overlook minor and accidental

---

5. Proverbs 19:11.

offenses, confront humbly and lovingly, and forgive quickly and fully. Not every spark should become a forest fire and the grace of prevention is often the key suppressant.

James: Unfortunately, long-term relationships nearly always involve personal offense. My friendships today are shaped by an incident I caused many years ago with a friend that included a number of poor responses. Bothered by my friend's persistent tardiness, I made the mistake of using a passive-aggressive move to rectify the situation. To make matters worse, I didn't pursue peace through reconciliation when my friend caught on to my strategy and addressed the situation. Instead, I tried to minimize the moment and quickly end the uncomfortable conversation so we could move on. By God's grace we put the minor conflict behind us to remain close friends. However, as I look back, I can see opportunity for more grace in the beginning by overlooking what bothered me, in the middle by addressing it in a kind and helpful way, and in the end by pursuing peace through confession. In a sinful world, we cannot avoid personal offense. Therefore, we must learn to give and receive forgiveness easily to continue in peace.

## 8. Pray for each other

Prayerlessness is rampant in many, if not most, churches today. While this statement deserves a book-length defense and response, the results of this deficiency are seen in failed and fractured relationships all around us. One of the simplest and most fruitful contributions we can make to friendship is to pray regularly for our friends as God will use it to stir love and loyalty in our hearts for them.

Brian: When I consider those pastoral friendships that mean the most to me, it isn't gauged by how much time I spend with them or how much they have sacrificed for me. It is more based on their intentional efforts to pray for me when I least expect it. I remember a season of being overwhelmed with ministry that created a deep sense of loneliness. I found myself asking, 'Did anyone actually care about me, or only want something from me?' In a very low moment while driving down the road, I received an unexpected phone call from a friend. I answered and he said, 'Hey, I don't need anything from you, I was just thinking about you and wanted to know how you were doing, that I love you, and how I could pray for you?'

I began to weep while driving down the road and I had no idea why. I realized later I was deeply longing for someone to not need anything from me, but simply wanted to care for me. I learned something important about myself that day, but I also learned what I needed in pastoral friendship—being loved for who I am, not what I can do for you.

I have learned this is a deep longing for many pastors whose calling is to pour out so much for others. This longing in part can be filled with meaningful, reciprocal pastoral friendships. This experience also created a longing in my heart to want to be the same friend to others this friend had been to me that day. As a result, much of my ministry rhythm became sending random text messages to pastor friends and calling others on the phone when they least expected it to say, 'I love you. I was thinking of you. And I wanted to know how I could pray for you.'

## 9. Know your capacity and invest wisely

Seasons and spheres underwrite our ability to befriend, but none eliminate it. Each stage of life presents challenges to navigate and creates relational circles. Acknowledge and appreciate the nature of your present situation and give yourself to friendship with skill and deftness.

James: Three of the men I would consider my 'best' friends are disconnected from my day-to-day life because of distance. At various times in the past, we shared a great deal of time working or serving together in a local church and investing significant relational time together. But as life took us in different directions, the opportunity for intimacy diminished. In addition, the growth of our families and the increase of work responsibilities and demands reduced our margin and prevented us from cultivating those relationships despite the distance. Finally, we developed closer relationships with men who were more intertwined with our present lives. With limited resources to invest, we need wisdom to adjust our investment to focus on friendships that will most faithfully bless those nearest to us and bear fruit in our lives. While keeping a tie with old friends is important, we must evaluate and adjust the time and energy we devote to different friendships to protect the priorities at every stage of life.

## 10. Don't give up

For the sake of your soul, your family, and your congregation, persevere in friendship. If you look back, the past may well be a discouraging trail of disappointment with friendships you fractured, some that never formed, and others that ended in betrayal. God is working to shape and sanctify you, and He is able to provide friendships regardless of your age or past experience.

James: I have a few friendships that stretch back more than two decades, and I hope I was always a 'good friend.' Yet, God worked in me during my thirties to help me significantly in this area by growing in me an awareness and understanding of the nature and blessing of friendship. In fact, as I grow older, I can see evidence of His grace in giving me deeper and richer relationships by helping me to more wisely invest in them. As I reflect on God's blessings through friendship in the past ten years, I can list more than a dozen men of varied ages who I wouldn't hesitate to call on as a friend on any given day. To be clear, this blessing is owing to the grace of God and His faithfulness to me. Let your confidence in God's power and the testimony of our collective experience spur you on. Don't despair, brother, regardless of what lies behind; press on.

Even if we had the finest ingredients in our respective home kitchens, no one is awarding us a Michelin star anytime soon. The reason is simple: it's one thing to have the necessary components, but it's another to put them to proper use. Our prayer is that God will use this book to encourage and equip you for the investment in friendship and through that work bring the blessing of it home in your life.

# Conclusion
## 'James Brian and James Brian'

I (James) don't think I'll forget the moment I realized the personal detail we have in common. I was taking in Brian's office at the new headquarters of Practical Shepherding a few years ago while he was working on some coffee for us. He and I had developed a solid friendship already, which included co-authoring a book and hundreds of hours together. As I glanced over his Gospel Ministry License[1] I did a double-take. I skimmed the information on the framed certificate almost mindlessly, so my brain registered it in a way that shocked me. I immediately wondered, why did he have a copy of my certificate on his wall? Of course, he did not. My confusion was caused because his name—*James Brian Croft*—bears striking resemblance to mine, *James Brian Carroll*. Because our names are relatively common, sharing first and middle names with one another

---

1. In our church tradition, licensing is a common instrument for a local church to affirm a young man's fitness for ministry near the outset of his pursuit of it. For example, often a man's home church will license him as he leaves to pursue theological education and training.

is not all that rare. But it was surprising because it was unknown to me for so long in our friendship. While the fact may not seem remotely interesting to anyone else, I raise it because it illustrates a characteristic of our friendship that makes it a special gift to me.

The distinction is the combination of significant overlap mixed with enough variation to give us different perspectives. Our friendship began with two events. To the first, I came in a near emotional crawl and from the second, I left with a new resource for spiritual and emotional strength. Both meetings are still bearing fruit in my life today in large part because they are connected to the lasting friendship they produced.

The first of these is when I met Brian. I attended an event where I heard him tell the story of his first five years as Pastor of Auburndale Baptist Church. While there were substantial differences between the two churches we served, his description of the experience resonated with me and the testimony of God's faithfulness to sustain him and strengthen him to persevere encouraged my heart. God would use the time I spent listening to his story as a pivot point and now a marker in my commitment to persevere at Parkway Baptist (where I still serve). Although I trust God would have accomplished His purpose in my ministry without Brian, I am convinced he crossed our paths to provide an instrument of grace for me and for Parkway that has extended our time together. Further, God continues to use our shared experience of leading through change as a pastor in dozens of conversations over the years to bind our hearts and provide consistent encouragement to me.

The second occasion that solidified our friendship was a lunch together soon after that first meeting. My goal in connecting that day was to learn more about him and glean additional wisdom as he was a few years ahead of me in his pastorate. The meeting, though, quickly turned toward my background and the story of my life and ministry. Brian's ministry of listening to me that day and the follow-up to it would bear unexpected fruit in my life, relationships, and ministry for the next few years.[2] That conversation highlighted God's glorious grace, even in the differences in our lives, that led to similar pastoral ministries. Despite vast disparities in our families, educational backgrounds, vocational and ministry experience, training, and paths to pastoral ministry, we share a love for the local church, a desire to serve and edify her, and primary theological and philosophical commitments. That lunch served as a springboard for what continues to be a friendship that yields inestimable fruit in my personal life and ministry.

When I was first asked to consider joining this project, I wasn't quite sure. I was honored to work with these men but wondered what I would contribute. I've certainly learned through the process of reading their submissions and working to produce mine. However, more than any other outcome, this project reminded me that God's grace through friendship was an overlooked piece of my perseverance. To this end, we share more than a couple of names; we share a commitment to sharing friendship with one another and the importance of it with others.

---

2. The eventual result of that meeting was my first book, *Collateral Damage*.

*Also available from Christian Focus Publications...*

FOREWORD BY HARRY REEDER

# BIBLICAL CHURCH REVITALIZATION

SOLUTIONS FOR DYING & DIVIDED CHURCHES

✛

## BRIAN CROFT

ISBN: 978-1-7819-1766-4

# Biblical Church Revitalisation

*Solutions for Dying & Divided Churches*

**Brian Croft**

There is a unique and special power and testimony in not just a vibrant local church full of life, but an old historic one that had lost its way, was on life support, and into which God saw fit to breathe life once again. *Biblical Church Revitalization* calls us to an intentional commitment to church revitalization in the face of dying and divided churches.

*This book is a gift to pastors and church leaders who are yearning to see God do a work of spiritual transformation in a dying church ... Read it prayerfully and humbly, put its precepts into practice, and see God do what He alone can do—give life to the dead!*

Andrew Davis
Senior Pastor, First Baptist Church, Durham, North Carolina

*... an inspirational, instructive and insightful volume on how to minister effectively to churches that are dying, stagnant or declining.*

Harry L. Reeder III
Senior Pastor, Briarwood Presbyterian Church,
Birmingham, Alabama

BRIAN CROFT &
JAMES B. CARROLL
FOREWORD BY MARK CLIFTON

FACING
SNARLS&
SCOWLS

PREACHING THROUGH
HOSTILITY, APATHY, AND ADVERSITY
IN CHURCH REVITALIZATION

ISBN: 978-1-5271-0382-5

# Facing Snarls and Scowls

*Preaching through Hostility, Apathy and Adversity in Church Revitalization*

**Brian Croft and James B. Carroll**

Pastor, the hard work of church revitalization is a unique experience and battle ground. It can feel like you're all alone. But the trials you face are not new. Faithful preachers throughout scriptures and church history have encountered hostility, apathy, and adversity, and continue to do so today. Brian Croft and James Carroll share their personal stories and seek to encourage you to faithfully persevere in this Spirit-empowered, God-honoring, Christ-exalting work.

*It seems I have read enough books on preaching to populate a small book store, but never one like this. Both authors have served as faithful preachers in a revitalizing context for many years and have long practiced the things they write about here. Read it and be reminded (and instructed) that the power of God for transformation—for the church—lies in what the apostle Paul calls 'the foolishness of preaching.'*

Jeff Robinson
Pastor, Christ Fellowship Church of Louisville, Kentucky and
Senior Editor, The Gospel Coalition

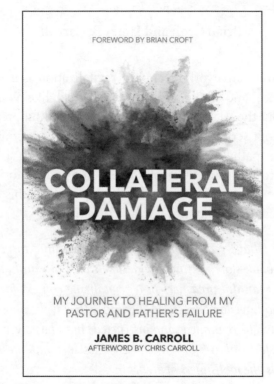

FOREWORD BY BRIAN CROFT

# COLLATERAL DAMAGE

MY JOURNEY TO HEALING FROM MY
PASTOR AND FATHER'S FAILURE

**JAMES B. CARROLL**
AFTERWORD BY CHRIS CARROLL

ISBN: 978-1-5271-0003-9

# Collateral Damage

*My Journey to Healing from my Pastor and Father's Failure*

**James B. Carroll**

At twelve years old, James Carroll became the collateral damage of his pastor father's infidelity and his parents' divorce. With his world completely shaken and identity in shreds, he could hardly process what was happening, let alone begin regaining normality. In *Collateral Damage*, Carroll, now a pastor himself, presents the specific ways in which God has worked in his life during and since that time—healing wounds, revealing sin, and restoring life. This is a highly practical book, showing the gospel as the power of God to save, to restore, and to heal.

*Every soul is broken by personal sin and the consequences of others' sin and every Christian is called to minister to broken souls, beginning with his or her own. Carroll's book is a consecrated prescription to follow.*

Paul Chitwood
President, International Mission Board of the
Southern Baptist Convention

*About good news in pain, hope in anguish, and power in reconciliation. You cannot read this book without loving God and His church even more.*

Chuck Lawless
Dean and Vice-President of Graduate Studies and Ministry
Centers, Southeastern Baptist Theological Seminary, Wake Forest,
North Carolina

EARLY CHURCH FATHERS
SERIES EDITOR MICHAEL A. G. HAYKIN

# PATRICK

## OF IRELAND

### HIS LIFE & IMPACT

MICHAEL A. G. HAYKIN

ISBN: 978-1-5271-0100-5

# Patrick of Ireland

*His Life and Impact*

**Michael A. G. Haykin**

Patrick ministered to kings and slaves alike in the culture that had enslaved him. Patrick's faith and his commitment to the Word of God through hard times is a true example of the way that God calls us to grow and to bless those around us through our suffering. Michael Haykin's masterful biography of Patrick's life and faith will show you how you can follow God's call in your life.

*Michael Haykin paints a compelling portrait of this bibliocentric bishop and earnest evangelist. The dedicated missionary and thoughtful theologian that emerges belongs to the Gospel-loving global church and not just the Emerald Isle.*

Paul Hartog
Professor of Theology, Faith Baptist Theological Seminary,
Ankeny, Iowa

*Beautifully detailed portrait in miniature... all Christians will benefit from learning more about this mighty figure in the great cloud of witnesses.*

Lewis Ayres,
Professor of Historical Theology, Durham University,
Durham, England

# Christian Focus Publications

Our mission statement —

STAYING FAITHFUL

In dependence upon God we seek to impact the world through literature faithful to His infallible Word, the Bible. Our aim is to ensure that the Lord Jesus Christ is presented as the only hope to obtain forgiveness of sin, live a useful life and look forward to heaven with Him.

Our books are published in four imprints:

### CHRISTIAN
## FOCUS

Popular works including biographies, commentaries, basic doctrine and Christian living.

### CHRISTIAN
## HERITAGE

Books representing some of the best material from the rich heritage of the church.

## MENTOR

Books written at a level suitable for Bible College and seminary students, pastors, and other serious readers. The imprint includes commentaries, doctrinal studies, examination of current issues and church history.

## CF4•K

Children's books for quality Bible teaching and for all age groups: Sunday school curriculum, puzzle and activity books; personal and family devotional titles, biographies and inspirational stories — because you are never too young to know Jesus!

Christian Focus Publications Ltd,
Geanies House, Fearn, Ross-shire,
IV20 1TW, Scotland, United Kingdom.
www.christianfocus.com
blog.christianfocus.com